Fabrizio Granà

Redesigning Organizational Sustainability Through Integrated Reporting

Routledge
Taylor & Francis Group
LONDON AND NEW YORK

G. Giappichelli Editore

First published 2021
by Routledge
2 Park Square, Milton Park, Abingdon, Oxon OX14 4RN

and by Routledge
605 Third Avenue, New York, NY 10017

First issued in paperback 2022

Routledge is an imprint of the Taylor & Francis Group, an informa business

and by G. Giappichelli Editore
Via Po 21, Torino – Italia

Publisher's Note
The publisher has gone to great lengths to ensure the quality of this reprint but points out that some imperfections in the original copies may be apparent.

British Library Cataloguing-in-Publication Data
A catalogue record for this book is available from the British Library

Library of Congress Cataloging-in-Publication Data
A catalogue record for this book has been requested

ISBN 13: 978-0-367-52811-9 (pbk)
ISBN 13: 978-0-367-52809-6 (hbk-Routledge)
ISBN 13: 978-88-921-3375-4 (hbk-Giappichelli)
ISBN 13: 978-1-003-05849-6 (ebk-Routledge)

DOI: 10.4324/9781003058496

Typeset in Simoncini Garamond
by G. Giappichelli Editore, Turin, Italy

The manuscript has been subjected to the double blind peer review process prior to publication.

Redesigning Organizational Sustainability Through Integrated Reporting

CONTENTS

LIST OF FIGURES

Figures

Chapter two

Chapter four

Chapter five

Chapter six

Chapter 1
INTRODUCTION

In 1987, the UN Brundtland Report provided one of the most popular definitions of "sustainable development", which was defined as a "development that meets the needs of the present without compromising the ability of future generations to meet their own needs" (WCED, 1987 p. 45). Cohen *et al.* (1998) highlighted that this definition of sustainable development is part of a broader political discourse that has exposed the concept of sustainability and its components to manipulation and contestation. Laine (2005) also emphasised that the elusiveness of the definition provided by the Brundtland Report has enabled the concept of "sustainability" [1] to gain prominence in environmental and social discourse worldwide, since "it has been possible to define the concept to suit one's own purposes" (p. 397). According to Bebbington and Larrinaga (2014, p. 398), "while this definition is familiar to many, its radical nature can only be appreciated in the context of the time it was first promulgated" (see also Bebbington, 2001). In their view, "the broad nature of the Brundtland Report definition of sustainable development has allowed a wide coalition to unite under its rhetoric while the implications that arise from its application in particular situations remain contested" (2014, p. 400).

Following the Brundtland Report, institutions and international bodies have further attempted to specify what sustainability means and have tried to capture its main components. For example, at the Johannesburg World Summit in 2002, 'sustainable development' was defined as embracing not only environmental aspects but social inclusion and economic development as well (see Drexhage and Murphy, 2010). This definition was further reinforced in 2012 by the United Nations and extended in 2013 by the Sustainable Development Solutions Network (SDSN) with the inclusion of good

---

[1] As argued by some scholars, although *sustainability* and *sustainable development* are two distinct concepts, these terms are often used interchangeably and as being synonymous with other notions such as "social responsibility" or "environmental management" (Gray, 2010; Lozano, 2008; Han Onn and Woodley, 2014). Therefore, this book uses the expressions *sustainability* and *sustainable development* as two analogues.

governance as the fourth pillar and the publication of the Sustainable Development Goals.

The academic literature has also attempted to provide various definitions for the concept of sustainability (more than 70 according to Lozano and Huisingh, 2011). In this respect, Han Onn and Woodley (2014) emphasised that the number of definitions provided, as well as the different ways in which they have been operationalized within organizations, have left the term 'sustainability' basically undefined.

According to Frame and O'Connor (2011), the lack of definition of sustainability does not necessarily imply that sustainability also lacks meaning. Instead, the lack of a specific definition renders this concept an 'empty signifier', open to multiple meanings. This idea implies that, rather than remaining empty and therefore without meaning, the concept of sustainability can be filled with different meanings that are always evolving. Consequently, not only can 'sustainability' be defined in several different ways, but its components are also subject to multiple interpretations and definitions (Frame and O'Connor, 2011; Tregidga, 2011; Tregidga *et al.* 2012, 2014).

According to Tregidga *et al.* (2011), sustainability is more than an *empty signifier*. It is a *floating* signifier since it is overwhelmed with meanings; it is overdetermined – overfilled with so many different details, making it a universal concept (*empty*). As such, different social 'constructions' of the meaning of sustainability are possible since this concept can be filled with different content by various subjects. In this sense, sustainability means different things in the various contexts in which its meaning is constructed, and of which it is a part (Gray, 2010).

Giovannoni and Quattrone (2017) argue that, intrinsically, definitions are never bounded. They are "inescapably 'de-fined', that is, never fully spatially and categorically closed" (p. 52). Therefore, the absence of a bounded definition does not lead to absolute emptiness or nothingness for a concept that is poorly defined, but rather it provides the possibility for this concept to be filled with meanings that are constantly unfolding. It follows that 'sustainability' is not meaning*less* because it lacks a definition (as also suggested by Cohen *et al.*, 1998; Frame and O'Connor, 2011). On the contrary, it is this lack (or 'absence' – Giovannoni and Quattrone, 2017) that provides the conditions for sustainability to become meaning*ful* as it is filled with multiple and unfolding meanings.[2]

[2] In this book, the adjective "meaningful" is literally defined as being "full of meaning". The etymology of the adjective "meaning*ful*" results from the combination of two separate words – "meaning (n.) + –ful" – and is opposed to the adjective "meaning*less*",

At the corporate level, the ambiguity of the concept of sustainable development/sustainability, and the consequent plurality of meanings it can be associated with, have enabled organizations to capture this concept 'for their own ends' with continuing negative outcomes (Tregidga *et al.* 2018, p. 295).

Such plurality has rendered "sustainable development" a hegemonic discourse, within which one empty concept is replaced by another one, empty enough to attract, accommodate and gain consensus among a range of particulars (Tregidga *et al.* 2018, p. 313).

Along these lines, a number of studies emphasise that sustainability reporting practices are often used as a means for covering, rather than uncovering, corporate social and environmental impacts (Gond *et al.* 2009; Cho *et al.* 2010; Milne and Gray, 2013).

Cho *et al.* (2010) emphasized that organizations' reputational pressures and search for legitimacy may generate distortions on sustainability reporting, as managers try to deflect, obfuscate, or alter information on social and environmental performance (see, also, Cho *et al.*, 2015; Gond *et al.* 2009; O'Dwyer *et al.*, 2005; Burritt and Schaltegger, 2010; Hopwood, 2009).

Most of the literature mentioned above concentrates on the practices for representing, reporting, and accounting for sustainability, and on the need for reducing the gap between what companies actually *do* and what they *say* about sustainability. However, other studies maintain that this gap does not necessarily have distortive effects (Christensen *et al.* 2013; Christensen *et al.* 2015; Guthey and Morsing, 2014). Likewise, a number of studies suggest that further exploration is needed to explain what ongoing attempts to represent sustainability (its represent*ing*) produce in practice within an organization (see for example Busco and Quattrone, 2015; Quattrone, 2015; 2017).

Cho *et al.* (2015) build on prior studies on organized hypocrisy and organizational façade to explore the discrepancies between corporations' talk decisions and actions, and emphasise the enabling effects of these discrepancies. They argue that organizational façades and organized hypocrisy may enable greater flexibility in managing stakeholders' expectations and provide opportunities for action through the aspirations that they entail (Cho *et al.*, 2015).

This point is further expanded by Gibassier *et al.* (2017) in relation to integrated reporting. By drawing on the work of Busco and Quattrone (2015), Gibassier *et al.* (2017) argued that innovations such as integrated

---

which literally mean "devoid of meaning". This interpretation is not distant from the widely accepted understanding of the adjective "meaningful", as generally related to something "intended to show meaning" (Cambridge Dictionary).

reporting stimulate action through the promises held by their mythical dimension, even if these promises are never fulfilled. In this sense, integrated reporting is 'aspirational' as it praises an imaginary future which stimulates more tailored accounting practices.

By relying upon these studies and, in particular, on the recent development of integrated reporting, this research argues that the ambiguity of sustainability as a concept, and the impossibility to fully capture it through accounting and reporting practices, does not mean that any attempt to represent it inevitably leads to distortion or obfuscates 'reality'. Rather, the way in which this concept is presented through accounting and reporting practices can have a constructive effect on the organization through the aspirations that these representations entail.

In particular, even though it may be impossible for the concept of sustainability to achieve closure and therefore be 'de-fined', the ongoing attempt to represent *it* (and give *it* meaning) within an organization may lead to multiple 'discourses' about sustainability (i.e. different ways of talking about, understanding and interpreting its content), which may inspire new actions and interpretations of sustainability (Christensen *et al.* 2013; 2015).

Recent researches suggest that more academic and practitioners' studies are needed to understand the factors and motives underpinning the production of organizational messages of sustainability. For instance, as argued by Tregidga *et al.* (2012), "while further studies concentrating on the message are important, when investigating notions such as sustainability or sustainable development, for example, it is necessary to go beyond the message to include its production and consumption" (p. 228). Therefore, studies are needed for analysing the construction of the message, looking at the instances that come up when deciding 'what is to be said' and 'how it is to be said'. Further, Tregidga *et al.* (2012) maintain that "more studies analysing the notions of meaning, quality and accountability in organizational reporting and communication are needed because an examination of how organizational reporting and communication is constructed and its potential consequences (both intended and unintended) remains underdeveloped" (p. 228).

1.1. Research objectives

This study aims *to explore the role of accounting and reporting practices, such as corporate and integrated reports, as organizations attempt to represent sustainability.*

Whereas the majority of prior studies have discussed the representational ability of accounting and reporting practices, maintaining that a gap exists between "what companies say" and "what they do" about sustainability, this study maintains that the attempt to represent this concept, and give it meaning, may produce valuable effects. This study explores how organizations' attempts to represent sustainability (i.e. its represent*ing* – the process of representation) affect the way in which organizations understand and report on sustainability, changing its meaning over time.

In particular, this research examines whether and how accounting and reporting practices provide the conditions for the concept of sustainability to be filled with meanings. Further, it explores how these meanings unfold, eventually leading to evolving accounting and reporting practices.

To achieve the objective described above this research relies on the analysis of the sustainability and integrated reports published by DAPHNE[3], a multinational company that specializes in the production and marketing of oil and gas, from 1996 to 2015.

DAPHNE's sustainability reports have been classified in three periods (from 1996 to 2005; from 2006 to 2009; from 2010 to 2015) to explore how the meaning of sustainability evolved and changed over the years. For each period, the analysis focused on the concept of sustainability, exploring how it was represented through the reports, the meanings that emerged, the main external contingencies that influenced the evolution of sustainability reporting within DAPHNE, the key practices used, and the units responsible for the preparation of the reports.

The case of DAPHNE was chosen as a suitable site for achieving the research objective of this study because of its operating activities as an Oil and Gas company within the community, and the environmental resources with which it operates. Further, DAPHNE was chosen from a variety of companies operating in the oil and gas sector because of its role as a company leader in the pilot program launched by the International Integrated Reporting Council in 2010. DAPHNE's participation in the pilot programme has been considered a critical issue when choosing the case study for this research, because from 2010 the company's approach to sustainability reporting had radically changed by combining sustainability and profitability issues into a single process, and ultimately, into a single report.

---

[3] DAPHNE is a pseudonym used for reasons of privacy and confidentiality.

1.2. Contributions of the research

This study explores the representational abilities of accounting and reporting practices, and particularly integrated reporting, in relation to sustainability. This study argues that accounting and reporting practices are not expected to offer complete representations of organizations' sustainability. Rather, these practices offer a number of representations (e.g. graphs, diagrams, tables, grid) that affect the way in which organizations understand and report on sustainability, changing its meaning over time.

The analysis of the evidence collected suggests that the gap between what organizations say and what they do about sustainability still exists and cannot be completely closed because of the intrinsic incompleteness of accounting and reporting practices. However, accounting and reporting practices offer opportunities to discuss sustainability in several ways, thereby stimulating debates among different perspectives.

Finally, this study demonstrates that undefined concepts, such as 'sustainability', and practices, such as 'integrated reporting', mutually construct each other. The attempt to represent sustainability within the organization and the debates that this process generates, make accounting and reporting practices unfold themselves, and evolve.

1.3. Summary and structure of the book

The book is structured as follows. After the present introduction to the study, Chapter Two illustrates how the concept of sustainability has been interpreted over time, highlighting three main dimensions of this concept: the 'environmental', 'social' and 'business' dimensions. Considering the increasing necessity to understand the role of organizations in relation to the achievement of sustainable development, Chapter Two also describes the institutions and regulators that have contributed to the spread of sustainability reporting globally. Some critical issues regarding the implementation of the above initiatives are also described.

Chapter Three explores the inadequacy and incompleteness of accounting and reporting practices in representing sustainability within organizations. In particular, Chapter Three explores the main criticisms of accounting and reporting practices for sustainability, focusing on the opportunistic motivations that have moved organizations towards the adoption of sustainability, corporate social responsibility and integrated reporting.

Although organizations engage with sustainability issues to pursue win-win solutions, Chapter Three explores the potential that accounting and reporting practices, and particularly integrated reporting, have to motivate the different functions within organizations to develop and stimulate further action towards sustainable development. The objectives of the research are also described in Chapter Three.

Chapter Four illustrates the main theoretical underpinnings and framework used to interpret the research findings.

Chapter Five introduces the case study of DAPHNE and describes the research design, data collection and data analysis process, explaining the major challenges in conducting the 'empirical' component of the research for the analysis of the case study.

Chapters Five goes into an in-depth analysis of the material collected in order to achieve the research objective. In particular, Chapter Five provides a detailed analysis of the dynamics and contingencies through which the meaning of sustainability emerged and evolved within DAPHNE, also due to the accounting and reporting practices used to represent it. This chapter focuses on three reporting phases describing the main external contingencies that influenced the adoption of the reports, the meaning of sustainability associated with them, the key practices used and the units responsible for the preparation of the reports.

The research findings are discussed in Chapter Six.

Chapter Seven provides come conclusive remarks.

Chapter 2
DEFINING SUSTAINABILITY: THE EVOLVING DEBATE AND INITIATIVES FOR CORPORATE REPORTING

2.1. Introduction

During the past 40 years, the concepts of sustainability and sustainable development have been part of a broader political discourse, which have exposed their meanings and dimensions to manipulations and contestations (Cohen *et al.*, 1998). The debate on what it means to be sustainable has attracted the attention of a large number of national and international institutions, policy makers, cross-country initiatives and academics.

Sustainability and sustainable development are not considered to be two "static" concepts, that are stable in space and time (Gray, 2010), but refer to the durability and stability of dynamic processes in the long run, and implicitly integrate social, environmental and economic dimensions of present and future well-being (Stiglitz *et al.*, 2009). The durability and dynamism of the concept of sustainability, as well as its social, environmental and economic determinants, have often been interpreted in different ways (Drexhage and Murphy, 2010) and usually considered as separated by various researchers (Bebbington and Gray, 2001; Bebbington, 2009; Gray, 2010).

According to Lozano (2008), generally the concept of sustainability has been perceived as being highly "anthropocentric, compartmentalised, and lacking completeness and continuity" (Lozano, 2008 p. 99). In many other cases, the concept of sustainability has been considered as only focused upon environmental issues (e.g. Reinhardt, 2000; Drexhage and Murphy, 2010).

In this respect, Han Onn and Woodley (2014) emphasised that the number of definitions provided (more than 70 according to Lozano and Huisingh, 2011), as well as the different ways in which sustainability has been defined, have left this concept basically undefined.

Although significant effort has been expended on debating how environmental problems, social development and long-term economic viability are linked together within the concept of sustainability, it seems there is still no consensus on what sustainability actually means.

2.2. Defining sustainability

2.2.1. Sustainability as an environmental concept

The first relevant conception of sustainability emerged during the late 1970s and early 1980s when the term was associated with the need to protect the environment and natural resources. In this context, a growing concern for global environmental problems and scepticism about the possibility for reducing industrial pollution significantly (Meadows, 1972) pushed the United Nations (UN) to address these problems as a "barrier to development" (Kidd 1992, p. 16). One of the key steps in this direction was the UN Conference on Human Environment, which took place in Stockholm in 1972. The conference led to the development of 26 principles, most of which addressed the need for common principles for the protection of the environment.[1] The most relevant outcome of the conference held in Stockholm was the creation of the UN Environmental Programme (UNEP), an agency of United Nations that coordinates its environmental activities and assists developing countries in implementing environmentally sound policies and practices. In particular, the UNEP is responsible for the protection and improvement of the environment, climate change preservation and the safeguard of wildlife heritages and their habitats.

In 1979, the International Union for Conservation of Nature (IUCN), in consultation with the World Wildlife Fund (WWF) and UNEP, set up the World Conservation Strategy (WCS) to help advance the achievement of sustainable development through both the improvement of human life and the conservation of natural resources. The primary aim of the WCS was to promote sustainable development through the identification of priority conservation issues (Drexhage and Murphy 2010). In this context, the term

---

[1] http://www.unep.org/documents.multilingual/default.asp?documentid=97&articleid=1503

conservation refers to the "management of human use of the biosphere so that it may yield the greatest sustainable benefit to present generations while maintaining its potential to meet the needs and aspirations of future generations" (IUCN, WWF and UNEP 1980, introduction "World Conservation strategy").

The term *conservation* and its definition gained greater emphasis in 1987, when the report released by the World Commission on the Environment and Development (WCED), known as the Brundtland[2] report, provided the most popular definition of sustainability, that is, a "development that meets the needs of the present without compromising the ability of future generations to meet their own needs" (p. 45). The report was presented as a "global agenda for change" (WCED, 1987, p. ix) and identified sustainable development as the solution to the growing concerns over environmental degradation and the effects of the consumer society. The report was widely recognized by practitioners and academics as being the first official document that popularized the concept of sustainable development and positioned it as a topic of national and global importance, focusing on the reconciliation of the needs of present and future generations (WCED, 1987, p. 49). The attention given to the needs of present and future generations by the WCED's definition emphasized the importance of social aspects, and particularly, the key determinants of social equity.

2.2.2. Sustainability as a social concept

The United Nations Conference on the Environment and Development, known as the 'Earth Summit' in Rio de Janeiro in 1992, was the most significant event after the WCED in 1987. Not only was the Earth Summit a relevant moment for placing sustainable development at the forefront of many political agendas, but it created discussion among a broad number of stakeholders including world leaders (with nearly 100 world leaders and 172 nations represented), non-government organisations and some citizen representatives. Also, profit and non-profit organizations took part in the Earth Summit in 1992 as members of the World Business Council for Sustainable Development (WBCSD), formed in 1990 to give organizations the opportunity to participate in the process leading up to the Summit.

Since that time, a number of important international conferences on sustainable development have been held – including the Kyoto Conference on Climate Change in 1997, the Earth Summit+5 in New York in 1997 and

---

[2] The report issued by the World Commission on Environment and Development (WCED) is known as the "Brundtland Report, in honour of Gro Harlem Brundtland former Prime Minister of Norway and Chairman of the WCED commission in 1987.

the 2002 World Summit on Sustainable Development (WSSD) in Johannesburg. According to Drexhage and Murphy (2010), the 2002 Johannesburg World Summit on Sustainable Development (WSSD) "demonstrated a major shift in the perception of sustainable development – away from environmental issues, toward social and economic development" (p. 8).

This shift was strongly influenced by the release of the Millennium Development Goals (MDGs) issued by the United Nations (UN) in September 2001 and the necessity to encourage corporate social responsibility in developing countries. While the MDGs, in theory, applied to all countries, they were considered as targets for poor countries to achieve with finance from wealthier countries. The release of the MDGs aimed to provide a set of targets that were to be achieved by 2015 and to guarantee the respect of the rights and needs of the worldwide population, encompassing themes such as poverty, health and discrimination.

In 2012, a 20-year follow-up to the 1992 Earth Summit took place in Rio de Janeiro. The so-called United Nations Conference on Sustainable Development (UNCSD), also known as Rio+20, was aimed at securing renewed political commitment for sustainable development, by assessing the progress and implementation gaps in meeting the Millennium Development Goals, and also addressing new and emerging challenges. The establishment of the post-2015 goals was an outcome of the Rio+20 summit, which mandated the creation of an open workgroup that was to come up with a draft agenda. Within Rio+20 the UN agreed on the need for the release of the post 2015 MDGs, known as the Sustainable Development Goals (SDGs), by emphasizing the importance of both social and environmental concerns and the need for a more comprehensive definition of the role of business for sustainable development. The sustainable development goals (SDGs), similar to the previous MDGs, represent a universal set of goals, targets and indicators that UN members are expected to use to frame their agendas and political policies up to the year 2030.

The SDGs follow and expand the millennium development goals (MDGs). In fact, not only do they address some of the systemic barriers to sustainable development, but they also offer better coverage of, and balance between, the three dimensions of sustainable development – social, economic and environmental – and institutional/governance aspects (ICSU, ISSC; 2015). The goals are applicable in developing and developed countries alike. Governments can translate them into national action plans, policies, and initiatives that reflect the different realities and capacities their countries possess. Different from the MDGs, the SDGs are designed to engage a wide range of organizations and shape priorities and aspirations for sustainable development efforts around a common framework. Most importantly, the

SDGs recognize the key role that business organizations can play in achieving them (for a in depth review on SDGs see Busco, Granà, Izzo, 2018).

2.2.3. Sustainability as a business concept

The growing public awareness of environmental and social development has made broader sustainability concerns an inherent challenge for business (See Bebbington and Larrinaga, 2014). Since the release of the Brundtland report and the Rio Summit, sustainable development has transitioned from being an interesting, yet at times contested, ideal to a concept that enjoys widespread endorsement by international institutions, governments, businesses, and civil society. Confronted with these pressures, since the early 1990s, organizations have begun to use their annual reports to provide information, initially, on their environmental footprint, and then later, on sustainable activities through their sustainability reports (Gond *et al.* 2012; Spence and Rinaldi, 2014).[3]

From a business perspective, sustainability has been defined as the ability of an organization to last in time, by looking at its financial performance as well as the environmental and social assets that compose its capital (Gray 2010). Business approach to sustainability aims to balance the short and the long-term supply and demand of resources. Thus, sustainability is meant as the ability of organizations to respond to their short-term needs without compromising the ability to meet future needs.

This view stimulated debate among different scholars on whether sustainability as a concept may be approached by organisations to support and balance economic, social and environmental growth (i.e. Elkington, 1997; Adams, 2008).

Different positions emerged on balancing economic, social and environmental issues. In particular, business positions on sustainability varied whether they refer to a "weak" or "strong" approach to sustainability (Gray and Bebbington, 2001; Hopwood, Mellor and O'Brien, 2005; Stiglitz *et al.*, 2009). The "weak" sustainability position does not question the present mode of economic development and views sustainable development as being compatible with some modified version of "business-as-usual" (Hopwood *et al.*, 2005; Stiglitz *et al.*, 2009). "Weak" sustainability expects that human produced gaps in the natural world, such as a lack of resources

---

[3] According to the KPMG survey of corporate responsibility reporting in 2015, the number of companies that now disclose and report information on their environmental, social and economic effects has increased exponentially (KPMG, 2015). This survey shows that 92% of the world's 250 largest organisations had issued some type of standalone CSR report (KPMG, 2015).

or damage to the environment, will be compensated by organizations' technological and innovative development. In this view, economic growth is part of sustainable development, producing a richer world that is more ecologically stable (Hopwood, *et al.* 2005). Consequently, the weak position considers the three aspects of sustainability (e.g. environmental, social and economic) as being related to each other, but fundamentally separate (Tregidga, 2007) (see figure 2.1).

Figure 2.1 – Venn Diagram representation of sustainability (Source adapted from Lozano 2008, p. 1839).

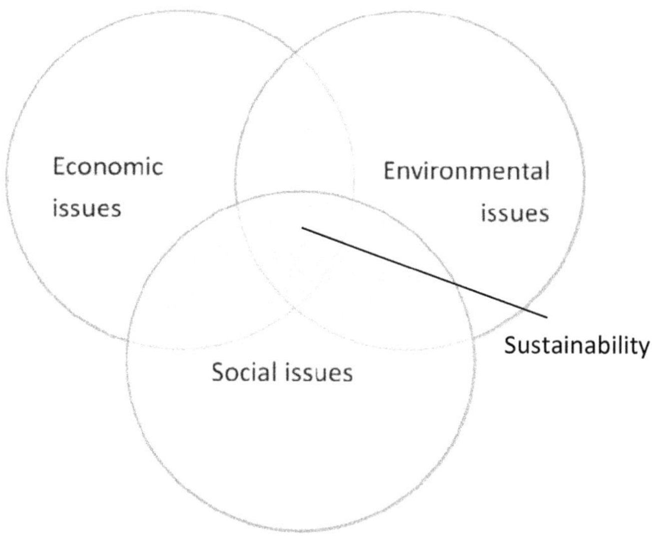

Conversely, the "strong" sustainability position points out that human capital and technological innovation cannot replace a multitude of processes that are vital to human existence, such as biodiversity protection, climate change or water management (Bebbington, 2001, p. 139). This concept of sustainability recognises the open nature of the interaction between social environmental and economic issues (Tregidga, 2007). In the "strong" sustainability position, the economy is not considered as being apart from society and the environment, but relies on these two elements, not only for its success but also for its existence. In the "strong" position of sustainability, the three elements of the economy, society and the environment are not separate entities, but instead, society is a subset of the environment, and the economy is a subset of both society and the environment (see figure 2.2). [4]

[4] In Figure 2.1, sustainability is represented at the centre and is surrounded by three

Figure 2.2 – Sustainability as concentric circles (Source adapted from Lozano 2008, p. 1839).

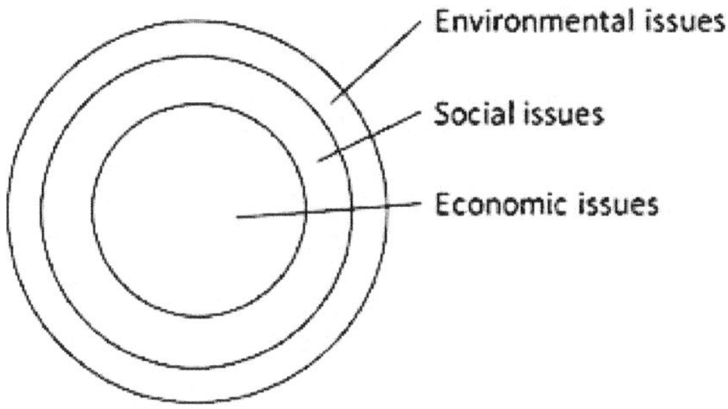

These representations have been criticized as considering sustainability as compartmentalized, without highlighting how the environmental, social and economic dimensions affect each other, limiting the concept of sustainability to a moment in time and consequently overlooking its dynamicity over time (Stiglitz *et al.*, 2009).

In this regard, other researchers have attempted to categorise business positions to sustainability using different models and representations, by looking at their different approaches (Hopwood *et al.*, 2005) and long-term orientations (Lozano, 2008).

For instance, Hopwood *et al.* (2005) map organizations different positions on sustainability, policy frameworks and attitudes into three main categories: The *Status quo*; the *Reform* and the *Transformationist* approaches.

The *Status quo* approach recognizes the need for change but sees businesses as being drivers towards sustainability, and economic growth as being a driver of sustainable development (Hopwood *et al.*, 2005). In this regard, Hopwood *et al.* (2005) explain that through the status quo approach there is a widespread perception that organizations increase information, changing values and new technology that may operate as the best means for

---

circles that are interrelated and represent the correlations between environmental, social and economic initiatives. In this figure, sustainability is achievable only if social, environmental and economic issues are met simultaneously (Lozano, 2008; Tregidga, 2007). Conversely, Figure 2.2 represents sustainability as resulting from three concentric circles with the largest representing the dimension of the natural environment and the second and third inner sub-circles indicating the dimensions of 'the society' and 'the economy' (Lozano, 2008). In this second representation, the environmental dimension has a predominant position in respect to the society and economy. Although these representations provide a basic understanding of the concept of sustainability, they suffer from various drawbacks and do not clearly explain the interacting relationships between social, economic and environmental issues (Lozano, 2008).

achieving sustainable development (Hopwood *et al.*, 2005).

The *Reform* approach accepts that the critical issues involved in current policies of most businesses, governments and trends within society (e.g. climate change; poverty reduction) need to be addressed, however, it does not consider that a collapse in ecological or social systems is likely, nor that fundamental change is necessary (Hopwood *et al.*, 2005).

The *Transformationist* approach, as the name suggests, seeks a radical transformation of society and/or human relations with the environment to avoid a mounting crisis or even a possible future collapse. In this regard, the Reform approach is viewed as being insufficient since many of the problems are considered as being located within the actual economic and power structures of society, hence they are not primarily concerned with human well-being or environmental sustainability (Hopwood *et al.*, 2005).

Lozano (2008) provides a further categorization of business positions to sustainability by stimulating reflections on organizations'"time" related orientations and their approach to economic, social and environmental issues (Lozano, 2008, p. 1838). In particular, he identifies the following five perspectives: *Conventional Economists*; *Non-environmental Degradation*; *Integrational* (i.e. encompassing the environmental, social and economic aspects); *Inter-generational*; and *Holistic* perspectives.

The *conventional economist's* perspective sees sustainable development as a further, desirable, economic development path. It is very limited in scope since it confuses sustainable with economic development, and thus neglecting the impacts of economic activities upon the environment and societies in the short, medium and long term. The *Non-environmental degradation* perspective represents an alternative way to consider industrialization's negative effects on the environment, valorising those activities that do not interfere with the overall environmental development. The *Integrational perspective* requires organizations to demonstrate how economic, environmental and social aspects of their activities integrate and affect each other (Lozano, 2008, p. 1840). The *Inter*-generational perspective focuses on the long-term effects of organizational activities, as the Brundtland Report suggests. The *Holistic* perspective explicitly combines the integrational and intergenerational perspectives, emphasizing two dynamic and simultaneous equilibria between "space" and "time" (Gray and Milne, 2002; Gray, 2010): the first one among economic, environmental and social aspects; and the second among the temporal aspects. i.e. short-, medium – and long-term issues (Lozano, 2008).

The nearly universal adoption of sustainability as a relevant issue of the viability and long-term growth of a business is, in part, due to organizations' awareness of its definitional flexibility and multiple interpretations.

However, the various views of sustainability interpretations aroused in the literature as well as the lack of clarity in its definition gives rise to ambiguity and conflicting views and opinions about what the outcomes of sustainable development are or what they ought to be (Joseph, 2012).

A number of critical studies maintain that a large part of this debate and the related confusion resides in the conceptual ambiguity of the definition of sustainability provided by the Brundtland report and the complexity of the objectives that it aims to pursue. Cohen *et al.* (1998) highlighted that the Brundtland report's definition of sustainability cannot be regarded as being 'scientific', but rather, as being part of a broader political discourse, which has exposed the concept to manipulation. Laine (2005) also emphasised that the elusiveness of the definition provided by the Brundtland Report has enabled the concept of 'sustainable development' to gain prominence in environmental and social discourses worldwide, as "it has been possible to define the concept to suit one's own purposes" (p. 397). According to Bebbington and Larrinaga (2014), "the broad nature of the Brundtland Report's definition of sustainable development has allowed a wide coalition to unite under its rhetoric while the implications that arise from its application in particular situations remain contested" (2014, p. 400). It is, therefore, possible to point to an array of issues that sustainable development concerns itself with, without coming to a formal definition that would encompass all possible activities that might arise within its ambit (2014, p. 399).

This has allowed both businesses and governments to be in favour of sustainability without making any fundamental challenge to their present course (Hopwood *et al.*, 2005; Laine, 2005; Gray, 2006; 2010), and has facilitated in the concept becoming rhetorical, making it meaninglessness and giving organizations and politicians the opportunity to use it as a catchphrase for demagogy (Hopwood *et al.*, 2005). According to Gray (2010), such demagogy and rhetoric also result from organizations' mistaken understanding of the concept of sustainability, which is mainly considered as a "system based concept and, environmentally at least… [that] only begins to make any sense at the level of eco-systems and […] difficult to really conceptualize at anything below planetary and species levels" (Gray, 2010 p. 48).

Further, after the follow-up Earth Summit in Johannesburg in 2002, not much appeared to have changed. Governments and businesses see sustainability as being a continued economic growth that has been made more environmentally sensitive in order to raise living standards globally and to reduce the gap left by increasing poverty and environmental degradation.

Despite organizations' recognition of and commitment to sustainability, the actions taken have not led to the core changes that are necessary for supporting a transition to sustainable development.

Various interpretations of sustainability have led to confusion in organisations and have compromised implementation globally (Gray, 2006). This has also given rise to an extensive debate about the nature and extent of information that organisations should provide and how they can measure, manage and communicate the social and environmental impact of their activities.

Further multiple institutions, NGOs and initiatives, as well as regulators, have tried to address these problems by providing guidelines, standards and principles regarding the ways in which organizations should report their environmental impact and progress toward sustainable development.

The following paragraph provides an overview of the most relevant frameworks and guidelines issued since 1987 for corporate social responsibility and sustainability reporting.

2.3. The need for a reporting framework: directives and initiatives on sustainability

Considering the increasing necessity to understand the role of organizations towards the achievement of sustainable development, national institutions and regulators have developed guidelines, principles and standards to enhance organizations' accounting and reporting in this regard. For instance, the UK introduced legislation in 2006 and updated it in 2013; Sweden adopted legislation in 2007; Spain in 2011; Denmark amended its legislation the same year and France in 2012.

In April 2014, the European Parliament passed a legislative resolution regarding the disclosure of non-financial information for large public-interest entities with more than 500 employees, (e.g. listed companies, banks, insurance undertakings and other companies that are so designated by Member States), in order to increase their transparency in communicating their environmental and social performance and, consequently, to contribute effectively to long-term economic growth and employment.

Building on some of the pre-existing developments listed above, at an individual country level in Europe, the European Union Directive 2014/95/EU requires that more than 6,000 large companies disclose in their management report relevant and useful information about their policies, main risks and outcomes relating to environmental matters; social and employee aspects; respect for human rights; anticorruption and bribery issues; and gender diversity in their board of directors. The aim of this regulation is to provide investors and other stakeholders with a more complete picture of an organization's financial and non-financial, as well as social, environmental and economic performance (European Commission, 2014). The first reports will be published in 2018 on activities of FY2017 (European Commission, 2014). According to the statement issued by the European Commission, the Directive 2014/95/EU provides technical content, but it is also important in cultural terms since the new directive attempts to increase transparency (defined by the Anglo-Saxon term disclosure) of business management (Eccles and Spiesshofer, 2015). The directive also aims to enhance consistency and comparability of non-financial information disclosed by organizations within the European Union, while respecting the necessities of organizations to use the most suitable international or national guidelines and approaches for sustainability reporting and corporate social responsibility (Eccles and Spiesshofer, 2015). In this regard, organizations retain significant flexibility for disclosing relevant information in the way that they consider most useful. They may use international, European or national guidelines according to the characteristics of their business or business environment (for instance, the UN Global Compact, Global Reporting Initiative or Integrated Reporting, etc.).

However, these guidelines vary widely in terms of scope, specification, issues covered, and methodology. For example, by providing guidelines to companies for sustainability reporting, the Global Reporting Initiative (GRI) has highlighted various dimensions of sustainability, (i.e. economic, social and environmental dimensions), which are to be included and disclosed within reporting activities. The multidimensional nature of sustainability reporting and the need for integrating financial and non-financial performance within the same report has also been emphasized by the International Integrated Reporting Council (IIRC). Considering its recent international growth and the relevance of its application to this area of research, Section 2.4 will explore more in depth the evolution and structure of the international integrated reporting framework issued in 2013.

The following paragraphs explore the relevant international initiatives and institutions that regulate the reporting of sustainability since its initial definition in 1987.

2.3.1. SustainAbility

SustainAbility was founded in 1987 by John Elkington, the creator of the so called "Triple Bottom Line" (TBL). Since the early 1990s, SustainAbility has been involved in corporate sustainability reporting, by focusing mainly on green consumerism and human rights, while evolving the concept of the TBL and helping companies engage with external stakeholders. The growing popularity of the TBL approach, and the authority gained by SustainAbility in the 1990s and continuing in the 2000s, both became key drivers towards the definition of sustainability as an integration of economic, environmental, social and economic aspects.

The notion of TBL was originally coined in 1994 and articulated by John Elkington in his 1997 book – *Cannibals with Forks: The Triple Bottom Line of 21st Century Business* – with the aim of balancing economic, social and environmental issues within organizational reporting in order to demonstrate their contribution to social and environmental responsibility. According to Elkington (1997), the TBL approach aims at guiding organizations to achieving a balance of economic, environmental and social issues. The traditional bottom line of the profit and loss account is not enough to take account of the full cost involved in doing business. So, through TBL, organizations are encouraged to add two bottom lines beyond the common measure of corporate profit to measure their social and environmental impact.[5]

From 1994 onwards, SustainAbility and the United Nation's Environmental Programme (UNEP) have collaborated together, through programs and publications, to explore a wide range of corporate sustainability challenges and develop guidelines. In particular, they developed the so called "Global Reporters Program", which produced several surveys on international corporate environmental and social reports, on the basis of an "ad hoc" benchmark tool used to interrogate the content of these reports. The benchmark tool produced by the UNEP/SustainAbility group has been revised several times since its development, making a few alterations to account for new developments in reporting (Chapman and Milne, 2003).

The earliest SustainAbility surveys covered environmental reporting, while only briefly exploring social issues. Then in 2000, the methodology underwent a significant revision. As part of the Global Reporters Methodology, SustainAbility took into account a growing consensus regarding various elements of economic, social and environmental reporting as it was emerging through the Global Reporting Initiative and various other corporate sustainability initiatives.

Although some difficulties have been identified with the UNEP/SustainAbility criteria, and although these criteria are being arguably sur-

---

[5] The traditional bottom line is the profit and loss account. The second bottom line considers how socially responsible an organization has been throughout its operations. The third measures how environmentally responsible an organization has been.

passed in terms of providing reporting guidance by the Global Reporting Initiative's frameworks and guidelines (which will be explored later in Paragraph 2.3.3), SustainAbility has been, and continues to be, an important element in the context of global sustainability reporting.

2.3.2. Institute of Social and Ethical Accountability (AccountAbility)

Established in London in 1995, the Institute of Social and Ethical Accountability (also known as AccountAbility) is a non-profit organization that brings together members and partners from business, civil society and the public sector worldwide. AccountAbility is a self-managed partnership, governed by its multi-stakeholder network and aims to promote accountability for sustainable development by developing innovative accountability tools and standards, most notably the AA1000 Standards series. From 1995, the Institute of Social and Ethical Accountability has developed a research network that studies and explores best practices in reporting for practitioners and policy-makers in organisational accountability, promoting accountability guidelines across professions as well as securing an enabling environment in markets and public policy. The first draft of the AA1000 standards was launched in 1999 to improve the accountability and overall performance of organisations by increasing quality in social and ethical accounting, auditing and reporting.[6]

According to AccountAbility, AA1000 standards comprises principles and a set of process standards. The process standards cover five main stages: Planning; Accounting; Auditing and reporting; Embedding; and Stakeholder engagement. In 2003, the Institute of Social and Ethical Accountability issued the first edition of the *AA1000 Assurance Standard* with the aim of assuring the credibility and quality of sustainability performance and reporting. The development of the AA1000 standards took over two years and involved hundreds of organizations, from professions, investment community, non-governmental organisations (NGOs), labour and business. The 2003 edition of the AA1000 standards, which superseded the first 1999 draft, was supported by a Guidance Note regarding the application of the principles and a User Note including some case studies on the application of the principles during assurance engagements. The 2008 edition of the AA1000 represents the second edition of AccountAbility's assurance standard. It draws on the growing body of practice and experience in sustainability assurance and supersedes all previous versions published by AccountAbility.[7]

---

[6] http://www.accountability.org/standards/

[7] https://www.accountability.org

In this regard, the second edition of the AA1000 standards focuses on the processes by which companies report on their impacts. This focus is based on the premise that unless, for example, corporate values are embedded, and unless governance systems, data collection systems, reporting mechanisms and audit processes are sound, reporting is unlikely to be representative of performance or reflect the information that stakeholders need.

2.3.3. The Global Reporting Initiative

One of the most influential international associations that provides guidelines for sustainability disclosure is the Global Reporting Initiative (GRI). The GRI was founded in Boston in 1997 as an initiative of the Coalition for Environmentally Responsible Economies (CERES), the Tellus Institute and the United Nations Environmental Programme (UNEP). The GRI is a long-term international initiative supported by multiple stakeholders, which aims to integrate sustainability within organizational decision-making processes and to empower decision makers through GRI's sustainability standards and multi-stakeholder network.

In 2000, the GRI launched the first set of Sustainability Reporting Guidelines. A revision process was then undertaken over the following two years, which culminated in the disclosure of the second generation of the Guidelines (G2) unveiled at the World Summit on Sustainable Development in Johannesburg. The 2002 Guidelines document presents a set of principles for the preparation of a GRI-based report. These Guidelines are for voluntary reporting and aim to assist organizations in representing a balanced picture of the economic, environmental, and social dimensions of their activities, products, and services.

Considering the increasing international interest in sustainability issues, the GRI launched its third generation of guidelines (G3) in 2006. Concurrently, the GRI launched a first version of the XBRL taxonomy for G3. Since 2008, the GRI released specific guidelines for a series of organizations and sectors (i.e. Financial Services, Electric Utilities, Mining and Metals, Airport Operators, Construction and Real Estate, Oil and Gas, Media, and Event Organizers).

Then in 2013, the GRI released the fourth generation of its Guidelines, G4, offering Reporting Principles, Standard Disclosures and an "Implementation Manual" for the preparation of sustainability reports by organizations of any size or sector. One of the aspects of the G4 guidelines is the materiality determination process, which outlines the four main phases of the process for determining the most relevant aspects that need to be included in a sustainability report (Identification, Prioritization, Validation and Review). The idea of sustainability as a multidimensional concept emerges clearly from

GRI's G4 Sustainability Reporting Guidelines – Reporting Principles and Standard Disclosure (2013), which highlights that "a sustainability report conveys disclosures on an organization's impacts – be they positive or negative – on the environment, society and the economy" (p. 3).

2.3.4. The Global Compact

The United Nation Global Compact (UNGC) was inspired by UN Secretary-General Kofi Annan during the World Economic Forum (WEF) in 1999 in Davos, Switzerland, where he challenged the top leadership of the worldwide business community to enact a Global Compact between the United Nations and the business community towards the observance of human rights, improvement of labour conditions, and protection of the environment.

The UNGC networks align business operations and strategies by following ten main principles, which focus on human rights, labour rights, environment protection, and anti-corruption (UNGC, 2011). In addition to making the principles an integral part of the business strategy and corporate reporting, local networks ask organizations to participate in the achievement of broader UN development goals, such as the Sustainable Development Goals.

Launched in July 2000, the UNGC is a leadership platform for the development, implementation and disclosure of responsible and sustainable corporate policies and practices. Endorsed by chief executives, the global compact is one of the largest voluntary sustainability initiatives, with 7,000 corporate participants in 135 countries, it also has 36,900 business participants, 9 governmental organizations (NGOs), governments and academic institutions. In particular, the UNGC platform embraces over 100 multi-stakeholder local networks (one per country), which are led by businesses with the aim of supporting organizations and creating opportunities for further engagement and collective action towards sustainable development.

The UNGC seeks to combine the best properties of the UN, such as moral authority and convening power, with the private sector's solution-finding strengths and resources, and the expertise and capabilities of other key stakeholders. The UN Global Compact offers a platform through which multiple stakeholders may interact to achieve sustainable development.

2.3.5. The Sustainability Accounting Standards Board

Founded in 2011 and based in the USA, the Sustainability Accounting

Standards Board (SASB) is a 501(c)3 [8] non-profit organization that aims at establishing industry-based sustainability standards for the recognition and disclosure of the most material environmental, social and governance impacts by companies that are traded on U.S. stock exchanges. The SASB validates the use of critical aspects of corporate sustainability performance for decision-making, supporting companies, investors, regulators and the public in addressing environmental, social and governance issues. [9]

SASB's vision is to share an understanding of corporate sustainability performance that would enable companies and investors to make informed decisions that would improve their outcomes on sustainable development issues.

In this regard, SASB aims to analyse the links between sustainability and financial performance through the concept of "materiality." Furthermore, the SASB has identified five broad categories of environmental, social, and governance (ESG) issues that can affect an organization's financial performance and, therefore, be highly material to investors. The materiality determination process cannot be fixed and varies from one industry to another.

From its infancy, SASB has developed a methodology for determining industry-specific non-financial material issues to which they have associated tailored performance indicators, derived from indicators that were already in use by companies. This methodology employs three main phases. During phase one, SASB's research team analyses the investor and economic impact of industry-specific material sustainability issues. Issues are then represented in a materiality map and are scaled, based on interest, financial impact, and a forward-looking adjustment (for emerging issues). As explained by Eccles and Serafeim (2013), each map prioritizes 43 ESG issues, ranking their materiality for a given industry on a scale from 0.5 to 5, with 5 being the most material. The higher the score for an issue, the greater its probable impact on an organization's financial performance (Eccles ad Serafeim, 2013). At the end of the first phase, an industry brief is issued, containing disclosure items and accounting metrics. Phase two involves the collection of feedback from over 2000 participants, such as corporations, market participants, public interests, and intermediaries, which are represented in an industry work-group. Their feedback informs an exposure draft standard containing accounting metrics

[8] According to IRS Publication 557, in the Organization Reference Chart section, the 501(c)3 correspond to the following type of organization: Religious, Educational, Charitable, Scientific, Literary, Testing for Public Safety, to Foster National or International Amateur Sports Competition, or Prevention of Cruelty to Children or Animals organizations.

[9] http://www.sasb.org/

and technical protocols for each material sustainability issue. In phase three, the exposure draft is released for a 90-day public comment period, and then the feedback collected is incorporated into the standard. Feedback is accepted for one year, at which time SASB releases an update and the standard is made available to the public.

By 2016, SASB had developed material maps and sustainability accounting standards for 10 sectors and over 75 industries.

2.3.6. The International Integrated Reporting Council (The IIRC)

The International Integrated Reporting Council (IIRC) is the most recent initiative that has been created by professional bodies and business-oriented networks to engage organizations in integrating financial and non-financial information, as well as economic, social and environmental reporting issues (Brown and Dillard, 2014). Launched in 2010, and formerly known as the International Integrated Reporting Committee, the IIRC was formed by the coalition of the Prince's Accounting for Sustainability Project (A4S) and the Global Reporting Initiative (GRI). The International Integrated Reporting Council (IIRC) is a global coalition of regulators, investors, companies, standard setters, accounting professionals and Non-Governmental Organizations (NGOs).

The IIRC's mission is *to establish integrated reporting (IR) and thinking within mainstream business practice as the norm in the public and private sectors.* In particular, the IIRC aims "to align capital allocation and corporate behaviour to wider goals of financial stability and sustainable development through the cycle of integrated reporting and thinking". [10] In September 2011, the IIRC released a Discussion Paper (DP) entitled, "Towards Integrated Reporting – Communicating Value in the 21st Century", which was a collection of suggestions and responses from producers and users of reports to be used as a basis for the development of the International Integrated Reporting Framework. This feedback was from a number of businesses and investors who had the opportunity to test the applicability of the principles, content and concepts of Integrated Reporting by taking part in a Pilot Programme that underpinned the development of the International IR Framework in the three years prior to September 2014. The IR Business Network had been created to promote integrated thinking among participants and give them the opportunity to access resources and expertise, to network with leading businesses, to gain relevant industry sector and expert perspectives, as well as share experiences and practices. Other networks cover the public sector, pension

---

[10] http://integratedreporting.org/the-iirc-2/

funds, technology, banking, accountants, academics, insurance and investors.

Following an analysis of the responses to the 2011 Discussion Paper, the IIRC released the first draft of the Integrated Reporting Framework on 11 July 2012. This draft was superseded by the Prototype IR Framework that was released in November 2012. During the development of the International Integrated Reporting Framework, the Technical Task Force of the IIRC organised Technical Collaboration Groups (TCGs) to prepare a series of Background Papers on the fundamental concepts (e.g. Value Creation, Capitals, Business Model) and Principles (e.g. Connectivity and Materiality) of IR. The background papers were produced in collaboration with the participants of the TCG, which were coordinated by lead organizations from a range of disciplines and countries. The IIRC considered interim findings from the TCG when preparing the Prototype Framework, released in November 2012, and considered aspects of this paper in developing its Consultation Draft of the IR, which was released on April 16th, 2013. After considering comments from stakeholders on the draft, the IR framework was issued in December 2013.

The framework provides the fundamental concepts, guiding principles, and content elements that govern the overall content of an integrated report. It does not focus on rules for measurement, disclosure of individual matters or on the identification of specific key performance indicators. Instead, the IR framework is principles-based rather than standards-based and is driven by integrated thinking. The idea is to recognize the wide variation in individual circumstances of different organizations, and at the same time, enable a sufficient degree of comparability across organizations (Busco *et al.*, 2013a).

The following section explores in detail the evolution of integrated reporting.

2.4. Integrated reporting

Originally labelled as "One Report" by Eccles and Kruzs (2010), the stated goal of IR is to provide information on financial and non-financial performance and their influence on organizations' value creation process in a single document (Owen, 2013). Integrated Reports include both qualitative as well as quantitative data, with the aim of offering a clear vision of an organization's business model, strategy, risk management and sustainable development (Adams, 2014; Busco *et al.* 2013a; 2013b; Dey and Burns, 2010; Owen, 2013).

According to the framework, an integrated report should provide concise information about how an organization's strategy, governance, performance, and prospects, in the context of its external environment, lead to the creation of value over the short, medium, and long term (IIRC, 2013 p. 33). An integrated report aims at describing the most material issues that affect an organisation and at enhancing accountability and stewardship, with respect to a base of six kinds of capital, or "capitals" (financial, manufactured, intellectual, human, social and relationship, and natural) (IIRC, 2013 p. 2). It provides information that fulfils the requests of a broader range of stakeholders (e.g. employees, customers, suppliers, partners, local communities, regulators, and policy makers), which are also interested in the organization's ability to create value over time (IIRC, 2013 p. 2). In particular, Busco *et al.* (2013a) highlights that an integrated report is not intended to be a set of multiple isolated pieces of performance information. Instead, it aims at embracing and connecting material information on financial and non-financial performance in order to show how value creation depends on multiples sources of capitals.

Although IR does not explicitly refer to sustainable development (Flower, 2015), it does focus on environmental, social and economic issues. In this regard, the IR framework, in Clause 2.39 explains that:

> [IR] supports broader societal interests by encouraging the allocation of financial capital to reward and support long-term, as well as short- and medium-term value creation within planetary limits and societal expectations (IIRC, 2013 p. 16).

Stacchezzini *et al.* (2016) argue that IR aims to extend the short-term focus of traditional corporate reporting to deal with a broad range of issues, resources and relationships considered material for an organization's long-term success and viability.

These issues, resources and relationship are described in depth through the Fundamental Concepts, Guiding Principles, and Content Elements issued by the International IR Framework in 2013. The following subsections provide a description of the fundamental concepts contained in the framework and then explores the guiding principles and content elements that should be debated throughout the process involved in the preparation of an integrated report.

2.4.1. Fundamental concepts

According to the International IR framework, an organization's value creation process is influenced by the external environment; created through relationships with other stakeholders; and, is dependent on the availability of various resources (IIRC, 2013 p.10). Consequently, IR seeks to provide insights about the external environment that affects an organization, the resources and relationships used and affected by the organization (e.g. capitals), as well as the way in which the organization interacts with the external environment and the capitals to create value over the time (IIRC, 2013 p.10). The fundamental concepts on which the integrated reporting process is built are (1) the capitals that an organization uses and affects, and (2) the value creation process.

According to the framework, all organizations depend on a different set of capitals, described as the stock of value that is increased, decreased or transformed through an organization's value creation process (IIRC, 2013 p.11). Six kinds of capitals are generally involved in the value creation process and can be classified as follows: financial, manufactured, intellectual, human, social and relationship, and natural capital. These are not fixed, rather they should be tailored according to the organization's value creation process and they ensure that an organization does not overlook a capital that it uses or affects (IIRC, 2013 p.12).

The second fundamental concept that lies at the heart of IR is the value creation process:

> "Value created by an organization over time manifests itself in increases, decreases or transformations of the capitals caused by the organization's business activities and outputs" (IIRC, 2013 p. 10).

The framework focuses on how an organization's value is manifest, not only in financial returns to providers of financial capital, but also in positive or negative effects on other capitals and other stakeholders (Busco *et al.* 2013a). The Business Model is the core part of the value creation process, and is represented as a chosen system of inputs, business activities, outputs and outcomes (IIRC, 2013 p. 13).

In Figure 2.3, the six types of capitals described above are both inputs and outcomes of the overall organization's business model. However, these capitals and their values do change over time, as they are increased, decreased or transformed through the activities and outputs of the organization.

The next section considers the guiding principles that underpin the presentation and preparation of an Integrated Report.

Figure 2.3 – The International IR Framework Value Creation Process (IIRC, 2013 p. 13)

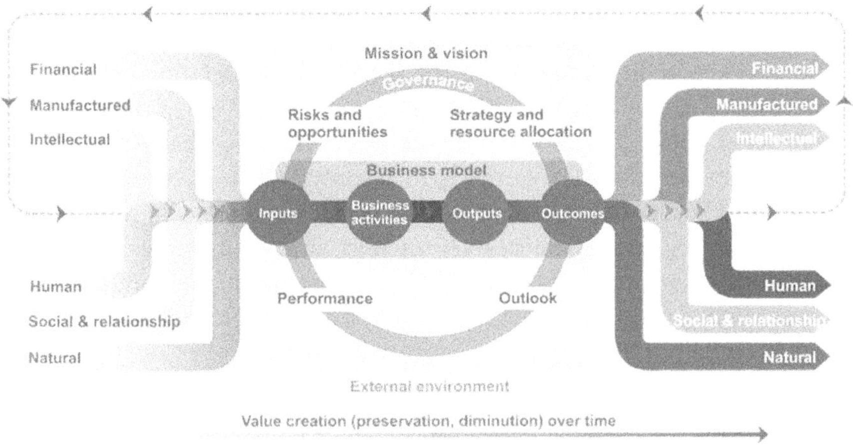

2.4.2. Guiding Principles

The six Guiding Principles presented in the International IR Framework are: "strategic focus and future orientation"; "connectivity of information"; "stakeholder responsiveness"; "materiality and conciseness"; "reliability and completeness"; "consistency and comparability" (IIRC, 2013).

The first principle, "strategic focus and future orientation", refers to the selection and presentation of a series of aspects that are related to an organization's strategies. It may include opportunities, risks and dependencies flowing from the organization's market position and business model; the relationship between past and future performance, and the factors that may change that relationship; the balance among short-, medium- and long-term interests and perspectives, as well as the evaluation of past performance that may influence future strategies. The framework explains how the implementation of the strategic focus and future orientation principle would enable an integrated report to clearly describe how the availability, quality and affordability of significant capitals that contribute to the organization's ability to achieve its strategic objectives in the future and create value (IIRC, 2013 p. 16).

The principle of "Connectivity of information" seeks to provide a holistic picture of the combination, interrelatedness and dependencies between the factors that affect the organization's ability to create value over time. This principle is associated with Integrated Thinking. The concept of "Integrated Thinking" is considered as being fundamental to the process of integrated reporting. It involves recognizing and managing all the capitals that the business owns and influences, considering the relationships between its various operating and functional units and the capitals that the organization uses or affects (IIRC, 2013).

First, integrated thinking lies at the base of the integration between various forms of capitals that an organisation uses or affects in its value creation process. This requires not only the achievement of stable financial results but also the allocation of the right resources such as ensuring suitable training for human capital; appropriate manufactured capital as well as ownership or access to the necessary intellectual capital; and explaining the correlations among them (SAICA, 2015). Furthermore, the evaluation of an organisation's activities, financial and non-financial performance and outcomes in terms of past, present and future capitals – is relevant.

Second, by building on integrated thinking an organization may improve its responsiveness to multiple stakeholders. Organizations should not focus on merely the achievement of financial performance but are also responsible for managing a wide range of stakeholders and interests.

Third, integrated thinking sets the conditions for an organisation to adapt its business model and strategy to changes in the external environment and safeguard its longer-term viability.

The framework emphasizes that the more integrated thinking is embedded within an organization's value creation processes and its activities, the better the connectivity of information flow between management reporting, analysis and decision making, and IR will be (IIRC, 2013 p.16). To achieve this connectivity of information, the integrated report seeks to connect the content elements and the fundamental concepts of the framework in order to communicate the overall organization's value creation story. Thus, the integrated report seeks to provide past- and future-oriented performance, financial and non-financial, as well as qualitative and quantitative information.

The principle of "Stakeholder responsiveness" reflects the relevance of creating valuable relationships among the organizations' key stakeholders. According to the framework, building reliable relationships with stakeholders may assist organizations in better understanding how stakeholders perceive value; identify future trends that may not yet have come to general attention, but which are rising in significance; identify material opportunities and risks; develop and evaluate strategy; manage risks; and implement strategic responses to material matters. Furthermore, the framework suggests that engaging with stakeholders on a regular basis should enhance an organization's accountability and transparency.

The fourth principle is "Materiality". The framework defines a matter as being material if it has "or may have, an effect on the organization's ability to create value. This is determined by considering effects on the organization's strategy, governance, performance or prospects" (IIRC, 2013 p. 18). The determination of materiality involves: identifying relevant matters based on their ability to affect value creation; evaluating the importance of such matters in terms of their known or potential effect on value creation; prioritizing the matters based on their relative importance and determining the information to disclose about material matters.[11] The framework explains that the materiality determination process is applicable to both positive and negative matters (e.g., opportunities and risks, and favourable and unfavourable results or prospects for the future), as well as to financial and non-financial information that has direct implications for the organization itself or that may affect the capitals owned by or available to others.

Another principle is "Conciseness". This principle requires that an integrated report provides enough information on the organization's strategy, governance, performance and prospects without being burdened with less relevant information. However, this is not synonymous with incomplete information.

The "reliability and completeness of information" highlights that an integrated report should provide the right balance between positive and negative material matters. The framework refers to reliability as the characteristic of a report that can be enhanced by mechanisms such as strong internal control and reporting systems, appropriate stakeholder engagement, and independent, internal audit or similar functions, as well as external assurance (IIRC, 2013 p. 21). According to the framework, senior management and those in charge of the preparation of an integrated report should exercise judgment in deciding whether the information is sufficiently reliable to be included in an integrated report. As for completeness, the framework suggests that a complete integrated report should include all material information, both positive and negative, that could affect the organization's ability to create value.

Then, "consistency and comparability" concludes the section dedicated to the description of the principles that underpin the integrated reporting process. According to the IR Framework, the information presented in an integrated report should be consistent over time and enable comparison with other organizations to the extent that the aspects reported are material to the organization's own ability to create value over time (IIRC, 2013 p. 23).

---

[11] For more detailed information on the Materiality determination process, please refer to the International IR Framework, pp. 18-20.

2.4.3. Content elements

An integrated report consists of eight elements that are relevant for communicating an organization's unique value-creation story (Busco *et al.* 2013a). According to the framework, the content elements of an integrated report are as follows: the organizational overview and external environment, governance, business model, risks and opportunities, strategy and resource allocation, performance, future outlook and the basis of preparation and presentation. However, the framework indicates that content elements should not be represented separately but linked together to better represent the story of an organization and its value creation process. The eight elements are not intended to serve as a standard structure for an integrated report. Instead, they should be tailored to an organization's individual circumstances. As highlighted by Busco *et al.* (2013a), such flexibility is key because it stimulates questioning and discussion about the most material aspects of the performance, prospects and governance of the business. For this reason, the IR framework Content Elements are presented in the form of questions, rather than being a checklist of specific disclosures (IIRC, 2013, p. 24).

The first of the content elements presented in the IR framework is the "Organizational Overview and External Environment". It describes the business and the circumstances in which it operates. An integrated report provides information regarding the organization's mission and vision and provides the essential context by identifying its culture, ethics and values; ownership and operating structure; principal markets; products and activities; as well as the competitive landscape and market positioning. Furthermore, organizations should report the main factors that affect the external environment including legal, commercial, social, environmental, and political factors (IIRC, 2011 pp. 24-25).

In terms of "Governance", an integrated report should provide insights on how an organization's governance structure supports its ability to create value in the short, medium, and long term. This should include information about the leadership structure; the specific processes used to make strategic decisions; the strategic direction and approach to risk management; how culture, ethics, and values affect capitals (IIRC, 2013 p. 25).

The "Business Model" represents the core element of an integrated report. According to the framework, the business model is the process through which an organization transforms inputs into outputs and outcomes through its business activities, with the aim of fulfilling overall strategic purposes and creating value over the short, medium and long term. An integrated report aims to describe the most material inputs of its value creation process and how they relate to the capitals from which they were derived. This includes key business activities, such as how the organization differentiates itself in the market, approaches innovation and adapts to change. Finally, outcomes describe how internal and external stakeholders perceive the organization's actions.

The content element "Opportunities and Risks" should define the key risks and opportunities that are specific to an organization, including those that relate to its effects on, and the continued availability, quality and affordability of relevant capitals in the short, medium and long term. The process of risk management is illustrated in the IR framework and is composed of three main phases. The first relates to the identification of specific sources of risk and opportunity, which can be internal, external or a mixture of the two. The second relates to the assessment of the likelihood that the risk or opportunity will come to fruition and the magnitude of its effect, if it does. The third phase requires that an integrated report illustrates the steps that are being taken to manage key risks and opportunities (IIRC, 2013 p. 26).

The fifth element described in the IR Framework is "Strategy and Resource Allocation". It seeks to describe where an organization wants to go and how it intends to get there. In other words, an integrated report is intended to inform users of the organization's short-, medium- and long-term strategic objectives; the strategies it implemented or intends to implement to achieve those strategic objectives; the resource allocation plans it has in place to implement its strategy; as well as how it will measure achievements and target outcomes for the short, medium and long term (IIRC, 2013 p. 26).

In the content element "Performance", an integrated report describes the extent to which the organization has achieved its objectives and how its outcomes have affected the capitals. As such, an integrated report should contain quantitative and qualitative information about performance on matters such as targets of risks and opportunities, the organization's effects on the capitals, the state of key stakeholder relationships and the links between past, present, and anticipated future performance.

According to the principle "Future Outlook", an integrated report should describe the challenges and uncertainties that the organization is likely to encounter and the possible effects of these challenges on the business model and future performance. In this regard, an integrated report should highlight anticipated changes over time and provide information on the organization's expectations about the external environment in the short-, medium- and long-term; how that will affect the organization and how the organization is equipped to respond to the critical challenges and uncertainties that are likely to arise.

Finally, the last content element "Basis of Preparation and Presentation", requires organizations to explain the way in which they have determined what elements to include in the report and the frameworks and methods used to quantify or evaluate material matters (IIRC, 2013 p. 29).

2.5. Challenges in representing sustainability within organisations reports

Despite the regulatory progress described above, the concept of sustainability has largely remained an idea and a not defined issue within organizations (Gray, 2006; 2010).

The multiple interpretations of sustainability, as well as the necessity to regulate it through different frameworks and initiatives, has given rise to further ontological and epistemological interpretations of the concept of sustainability, thus allowing space for organizations to misunderstand and misbehave (Gray, 2010). The problem, as Aras and Crowther (2009) suggest, is that the concept of sustainability is too broadly defined and insufficiently understood. As such, Gray (2010) affirms that through the interplay between the plethora of potential states of sustainability and the range of epistemological strategies that might be adopted within organizations, there is clearly no single "sustainability" that can be known and accounted for (Gray 2010).

Considering the variability of the guidelines adopted at an international and local level, Eccles and Spiesshofer (2015) are sceptical about the extent to which the consistency and comparability of the reports across the EU will be achieved after the implementation of directive 2014/95/EU. They point to the absence of homogenous standards for an organization's "expected behaviour" in relation to corporate, social responsibility. The variety of the possible guidelines that could be adopted represents a further challenge for the EU, especially in determining the audience of the reports (Eccles and Spiesshofer, 2015). In addition, consistency and comparability of the information reported are difficult to achieve. Although different initiatives and institutions aim at providing frameworks and guidelines for improving an organization's reporting and accounting, they have not provided much guidance for managers.

Largely missing from these efforts is a clear understanding of the very real trade-offs that exist between financial and sustainability performance. Although such aspirations are widely recognized and regulated by different initiatives and regulators (e.g. GRI, SASB, IIRC among other), organizations prepare sustainability reports with the interest of being financially rewarded for 'doing good', even when the issues they address are not relevant to their strategy or operations (Gray, 2010).

In this regard, according to Bebbington *et al.* (2008), although many organizations prepare their sustainability reports by adopting guidelines and frameworks that aim at representing sustainability issues within their traditional activities, these frameworks are used as tools for legitimizing their management decisions and actions (Bebbington *et al.*, 2008).

For instance, one of the most common criticisms of the approach to sustainable development through the GRI guidelines is that although it attempts to provide a holistic and balanced view of social, environmental and economic dimensions, it separates them (Moneva *et al.*, 2006, p. 132). In the absence of such integration, companies tend to provide information that is more controllable and related to the financial objectives of the organisation (Bebbington, 2001). Furthermore, the GRI has been criticized as it provides partial and incoherent guidelines to organizations willing to represent their social, environmental and economic issues within their accounting and reporting processes.[12] According to Moneva *et al.* (2006), GRI guidelines seem to simplify the concept of sustainable development into a collection of information on the indicators that comprise the Triple Bottom Line (TBL), which, instead of reducing the gap between organizations performance and impacts, tends to increase it (Moneva *et al.*, 2006). Similarly, Milne and Gray (2013) affirm that GRI's guidelines are partial and incoherent. First, they are partial in that the full range of social and environmental actions and interactions are incomplete – representing (in part) the difficulty of producing acceptable indicators and (in part) the reluctance of member organizations to sign up to indicators which are too demanding. Second, these guidelines are incoherent because "there is no apparent over-arching framework that guides the selection of indicators and ensures their relationships one to another and between the issues of concern and the entity" (Milne and Gray, 2013 p. 21).

SustainAbility benchmarking has been criticized in that it simplifies the concept of sustainability to economic, environmental and social issues without exposing the inherent conflicts and trade-offs between them (Gray and Milne, 2004). This has led to incorrect use of the TBL model – as used interchangeably with the concept of sustainability (Milne and Gray, 2013). Numerous other studies have been critical about the information reported using TBL, which is driven primarily by impression management purposes (e.g. Neu *et al.*, 1998); drawn predominantly to achieve win-win solutions (Gray, 2006) and unable to address the gap between corporate performance and corporate impacts (Milne and Gray, 2013). These studies are considered in more detail in Chapter three.

---

[12] For a further review on the concept of Triple Bottom Line (TBL) see Archel *et al.* 2011; Elkington, 1997; Milne and Gray, 2013; Moneva *et al.* 2006.

The principles of AA1000 have also been criticised for being excessively focused on the perspective of the organisation, raising concerns regarding the independence of the auditing function, which acts on behalf of the organisation (Adams, 2004; Milne *et al.*, 2001).

Although some academics and practitioners have described the potential benefits of implementing integrated reporting and integrated thinking in managing sustainability issues by integrating multiple capitals within organization's strategies, others have firmly criticized the role of the IIRC and its framework as being "a masterpiece of obfuscation and avoidance" (Milne and Gray, 2013).

Although IR is meant to mobilize large amounts of corporate information, facilitating engagement and activism from the organization's internal and external stakeholders, some critics have recently emerged (Eccles and Serafeim, 2013; Owen, 2013; Busco *et al.* 2013a). According to Milne and Gray (2013), the framework brings organizations and users "further away from any plausible possibility that sustainability might be seriously embraced by any element of business and politics" (Milne and Gray, 2013 p. 20). For instance, according to Humphrey *et al.* (2016), there is little indication in the materials provided by the IIRC about how and why integrated reporting meets the needs of a more sustainable global economy. Furthermore, they affirm that is not clear what exactly these needs are and who determined them (Humphrey *et al.*, 2016, p. 42).

For these reasons, Humphrey *et al.* (2016) maintain that such ambiguity about the aims of the IIRC, make integrated reporting an appealing idea not so much because of its innovativeness or because of its openness to various stakeholders, but because different parties and interest groups can all construct their integrated report in a way that makes it attractive to them. Furthermore, the lack of standards of IR for nonfinancial information makes different companies' performance difficult to compare, questioning the reliability, consistency and completeness of the information presented in an integrated report (Brown and Dillard, 2014; Flower, 2015).

Brown and Dillard (2014) criticize how the IIRC framework, as similar to other guidelines, seems to favour the lens of shareholder wealth maximization, emphasizing potential "win-win" opportunities for approaching sustainability within organizations. In this regard, IR provides a way of making sustainability impacts measurable in financial terms and aims at maximizing long-run shareholder value by indicating how an organization's mission, objectives, strategies, performance measurement systems and indicators integrate with each other (Brown and Dillard, 2014). Also, Flower (2015) criticizes the way in which the original purposes of the IIRC to support sustainable development has been abandoned and replaced by the concept of value creation in the final version of the framework. He criticizes the business-oriented approach of IR, which assumes that there is no conflict between the well-being of an organization and the society (see also Humphrey *et al.* 2016; O'Dwyer and Unerman, 2016).

IR adopters and users still face constraints on the determination of the information that an integrated report should contain, as well as their materiality for the overall organizations' value creation. For instance, Flower (2015) sustains that the IIRC concept of value creation is too vague and largely oriented towards an organization's investors' requests, rather than broader communities of stakeholders. Further, Flower (2015) emphasizes that an integrated report cannot provide a complete representation of the overall organization's value creation process as the content may be biased by the expectations of the shareholders, which may also affect the materiality determination methodology adopted. Also, the evaluation of the most relevant aspects that "have, or may have, an effect on the organization's ability to create value", and so of the capitals that an organization exploits or affects, may be biased to the extent that they are inputs to the organization's production process (Flower, 2015).

Likewise, Brown and Dillard (2014) argue that "integrated reporting (in effect, if not intention) seems more likely to reinforce rather than transform (unsustainable) status quo pathways" (Brown and Dillard, 2014). On a similar critical vein, Milne and Gray (2013, p. 20) view the IIRC's discussion paper, "Towards Integrated Reporting", as a masterpiece of "obfuscation and avoidance of any recognition of the prior 40 years of research and experimentation".

2.6. Summary and some further thoughts

The number of definitions of sustainability described in the literature, as well as the different ways through which these definitions are interpreted and described, have left 'sustainability' basically undefined. From this point of view, given its multidimensional and complex nature, it is impossible to capture all aspects of sustainability, since they require multiple bodies of knowledge and disciplines to be defined (Han Onn and Woodley, 2014). However, Bebbington and Larrinaga (2014) also emphasise that the lack of definition of sustainability has been a challenge for a number of initiatives and institutions that ground their usual mode of inquiry on well-defined categories and concepts.

Little prior research has focused on the organizational processes underlying sustainability accounting and reporting (Adams and Larrinaga-Gonzáles,

2007; Burritt and Shaltegger, 2010; Gond *et al.* 2012). Furthermore, little is known about the process through which organizations' construct their own approach to sustainable development and what the roles of accounting and reporting practices actually are, so that it can be meaningful within organizations. In this regard, understanding the process through which organizations' accounting and reporting practices are produced, as well as the quality and accountability of the information reported are all crucial in the examination of how sustainability takes form and becomes meaningful within organizations. The dynamics by which sustainability becomes meaningful through accounting and reporting practices is explained in the next chapter, together with the implications of these dynamics on the variety of accounting and reporting practices associated with "sustainability".

Chapter 3

REPRESENTING SUSTAINABILITY WITHIN CORPORATE REPORTING: CRITICISMS AND IMPLICATIONS

3.1. Introduction

Whereas many studies agree on the importance of organisations' addressing issues of sustainability, its ubiquitous nature and meaning leave the concept open to multiple interpretations, thereby allowing organisations to interpret sustainability in different and evolving ways (See chapter two).

Although the concept of sustainability as defined by the Brundtland report has been criticized as being "one of the most sophisticated notions" to define (Gray, 2006 p. 74), during the last 20 years it has turned out to be one of the most highly used terms within organisations' sustainability accounts and reports (Zappettini and Unerman, 2016). Rather than seeking to address the most profound challenges of connecting sustainability issues within tangible operations, organisations use accounting and reporting practices to combine good business performance with reasonable levels of corporate responsibility and selective accountability of their sustainability initiatives (Gray, 2006). For this reason, it is increasingly well established in the literature that a large part of reporting and accounting practices on sustainability have little, if anything, to do with sustainability itself (Gray, 2010; Milne and Gray, 2013). This chapter explores the role of accounting and reporting practices in representing sustainability issues within organisations, as well as their ongoing adoption in order to give meaning to sustainability issues within organisational strategies and initiatives.

3.2. Criticism of accounting and reporting for sustainability

Accounting and reporting practices for sustainability are usually regarded with suspicion by critical researchers. The lack of definition of the concept of sustainability has had negative implications for accounting and reporting practices, leading to criticism that it offers the opportunity for organisations to give misleading messages about sustainability performance (Gray and Milne, 2002; O'Dwyer, Unerman, and Hession, 2005; Gray, 2006; Cho, Roberts, and Patten, 2010; Gond *et al.*, 2009; Gray, 2010; Tregidga *et al.*, 2014).

According to Tregidga *et al.* (2014), although organisational references to sustainability are relatively commonplace in multiple reports, it is not clear how an organisation should behave in order to be 'sustainable'. Tregidga *et al.* (2014) draw on Laclau and Mouffe's (1985) discourse analysis to critically analyse how organisations construct their sustainable "identity" and represent themselves through corporate reports. By analysing more than 365 public corporate reports in New Zealand from 1992 to 2010, they affirm that statements about what a sustainable organisation represents are largely absent, giving different interpretations of sustainability. As mentioned by Tregidga *et al.* (2014):

> "The absence of statements stating what constitutes a 'sustainable organisation' could be interpreted as representing uncertainty around the concept. Alternatively, it could indicate that the organisations analysed [...] have not reached a position where they have conceptualized what it means to be sustainable, they do not directly align their current identity with that of a sustainable organisation, or that strategically, they avoid such precise expression" (p. 490).

As noted by Bebbington and Larrinaga (2014), not only 'sustainability' can be defined in several different ways, but also its components are subject to multiple interpretations and definitions, as "they are arenas which can only be understood through multiple lenses" (p. 399).

According to Frame and O'Connor (2011), the lack of definition of sustainability renders this concept an 'empty signifier', open to multiple meanings. This idea implies that, rather than remaining empty and therefore without meaning, the concept of sustainability can be filled with different meanings that are always evolving. This point is further developed by Tregidga *et al.* (2018). In their view, the nature of sustainability as an empty signifier renders it 'universal' but also open to multiple interpretations, as well as to the exercise of power by different groups of interests. In their view,

> "Attempts to fill sustainable development with meaning can be argued to be corporations' attempt to gain (or maintain) hegemonic control of the discursive space. The articulations of sustainable development can be viewed as hegemonic articulations that contain two seemingly contradictory features: certainty and vagueness" (p. 303)

By drawing on the work of Laclau and Mouffe (1985), they argue that the concept of 'sustainable development' act as a nodal point around which a plurality of other signifiers is articulated and ordered. At the corporate level, such plurality has rendered 'sustainable development' a hegemonic discourse, within which one empty concept is replaced by another one, empty enough to attract, accommodate and gain consensus among a range of particulars. Therefore, Tregidga *et al.* (2018) argue that:

> "[…] although sustainable development remains largely universal, the corporate discourse has partially filled sustainable development with a particular identity (economic-focused and profitable)" (p. 313).

It follows that the ambiguity of the concept of sustainable development/sustainability, and the consequent plurality of meanings it can be associated with, have enabled organizations to capture this concept "for their own ends" with continuing negative outcomes (Tregidga *et al.* 2018, p. 295).

According to Han Onn and Woodley (2014), the number of definitions provided, as well as the different ways through which these definitions are interpreted at the corporate level, have left 'sustainability' basically undefined. In this regard, a number of scholars have emphasised that the lack of a stable definition of sustainability has been a challenge for those disciplines that ground their mode of inquiry on well-defined categories (see Bebbington and Larrinaga, 2014), and has had negative implications for accounting and reporting practices (Gray, 2006; 2010; Gray and Milne, 2002).

The negative effects of the dominant, corporate-focused, sustainability discourse have been also emphasised by accounting studies. For example, Gray and Milne (2002) argue that current 'accounting for sustainability' practices fail to represent the cumulative effects of organizations' activities on the environment and society because these practices are mainly organization-centred, no matter what is the extent to which they are combined with information on social and environmental impact. According to O'Dwyer *et al.* (2005), sustainability reporting has remained limited in scope and unable to account for the rights, needs and empowerment of all relevant stakeholders. Similarly, Zappettini and Unerman (2016) contend that the term sustainability has been mixed and bent with other discourses to construct the organisation for the primary benefit of shareholders.

Albeit drawing on different perspectives, these studies emphasised the role of powerful coalitions in shaping sustainability discourses. From this point of view, along the lines of the 'hegemonic' dimension emphasised by Tregidga *et al.* (2018), the ambiguity of sustainability as a concept has enabled dominant groups of interests to maintain their powerful position also through the aid of accounting.

Further studies have emphasized that sustainability accounting practices have been often used as a means to veil past episodes of poor sustainability practices, rather than representing actual facts and managerial actions (O'Dwyer, 2002; Gond *et al.*, 2009; Gray, 2002; 2006; 2010; Milne and Gray, 2007; Spence 2007).

O'Dwyer (2002) interviewed a group of 29 senior managers employed by Irish public companies to study their motivations for undertaking sustainability reporting. Although a significant number of managers affirmed that their organisations' efforts towards sustainability resulted from a reaction to the market and the stakeholders' requests, most of the managers interviewed argued that the primary motives for sustainability reporting were dictated by the need to enhance corporate legitimacy (O'Dwyer, 2002).

Looking at the ideological implications and motivations that encourage organisations in approaching corporate social responsibility, Spence (2007) draws on Laclau and Mouffe (1985) discourse analysis to explore how Social and Environmental Reporting (SER) practices are constrained by opportunistic business as usual [1] approaches.

More specifically, Spence (2007) aims to link the motivations underlying SER with the images and representations of organisational socio-environmental performance. By interviewing representatives of 25 large capitalist enterprises in the UK, Spence (2007) criticizes business-based SER practices to be "antithetical" to the initial sustainability reforming intent to reduce poverty, and the inexorable ecological crisis. Such attempts have not been greeted positively by external stakeholders, but instead, have created scepticism about organisations' approaches to sustainability and the information reported regarding their social and environmental impacts.

According to O'Dwyer (2002), such scepticism is due to the tendency to provide poor quality disclosures, containing minimal information that are inconsistent with other data reported. Any additional data related to a so-

---

[1] At an organizational level, a 'business as usual' approach to sustainable development might be considered as a defensive strategy in environmental management, by attempting to limit, instead of focusing on ways to change and actions that would improve the environment. Under this approach, data is selectively reported. There is assumed to be little or no conflict between traditional economic and social or environmental dimensions of sustainability (Gray, 2006b).

cial or environmental issue is perceived as a form of "noise" that distracts managers from their primary objective of maximising economic returns (Gray, 2002, p. 370; see also Gray, 2006). Therefore, accounting and reporting are considered to be a poor tool for representing the cumulative effects of organisational activities on social and environmental issues and for supporting collective decision-making on such issues (Gray, 2002).

Research based on legitimacy theory has demonstrated that sustainability reports are used as tools through which organisations influence how they are perceived by the society, using sustainability disclosures strategically for window-dressing and impression-management purposes (Gond *et al.* 2009; Laine, 2005; 2009; Hopwood, 2009; Cho *et al.*, 2010).

By analysing the environmental disclosures of a leading Finnish chemical organisation between 1972 and 2005, Laine (2009) shows that sustainability reports are used as rhetoric and image management tools for strengthening the broader social beliefs on how organisations' business-as-usual has a mitigating effect on environmental problems and, thus, results in sustainability. He demonstrates that sustainability reports are used to exaggerate the external appearance and the reputation of an organisation, which may be rationalized and used to help it conform to social expectations (Laine, 2009, p. 1047). He maintains that organisations usually adopt win-win approaches to sustainability issues by focussing on actions that are seen to legitimately improve financial growth and shareholder value and contribute to the broader aspiration of sustainable development.

Gond *et al.* (2009) notes that the risk of adopting sustainability reporting for legitimacy relates to the use of accounting and reporting for "window-dressing" or as a means for building a better reputation for the organisation. Reputation driven reports and behaviours are developed in an attempt to make a good impression on external stakeholders without any underlying efforts to improve social and environmental welfare (Gond *et al.*, 2009). This contributes to increase the probability of organisations deviant behaviour towards sustainability objectives (Gond *et al.*, 2009), influencing external stakeholders and shareholders perception of an organisation's activity and giving more relevance to those accounts that have a strong reputational impact, instead of considering those that are of crucial importance or that are difficult to address (Gond *et al.*, 2009). Consequently, according to Gond *et al.* (2009) sustainability accounting and reporting practices do not necessarily promote socially responsible behaviour and are used as a means of building legitimacy and veil poor sustainability performance.

Accordingly, Hopwood (2009) maintains that organisations often use their sustainability reports to provide:

> "a new face to the outside world while protecting the inner workings of the organisation from external view. Done with skill and a fair amount of planning and thought, it is possible for some modes of reporting to thicken that veil such that even less is known of the corporation despite the apparent openness of its reporting." (p. 437)

The idea of corporate sustainability reporting as being a "veil" that hides organisations' misbehaviour, has been also acknowledged by Cho *et al.* (2015), who labelled organisations' sustainability reports as being merely "façades" of an organisation's poor performance that results in hypocritical behaviours[2] (Cho *et al.* 2015, p. 82; See also Spence, 2007). In another paper, Cho *et al.* (2010) emphasises how reputational pressures and the search for legitimacy generate distortions on sustainability reporting, as managers try to deflect, obfuscate or alter information on social and environmental performance. Using Fortune 500 data from the late 1970s to the year 2010, they show that organisations manipulate the information reported in their sustainability reports to emphasize good news and rhetorically deflect, obfuscate, or rationalize poor social and environmental performance (Cho *et al.*, 2010; 2015). In their attempts to balance ethical and legitimacy purposes, contemporary organisations maintain inconsistencies or gaps between what they state they have achieved and what they actually have done to achieve sustainability (Cho *et al.* 2015).

Even though the debate in the literature is still in its infancy, critical studies have looked at the most recent adoption of integrated reporting (IR) as a possible ceremonial response in search of a compromise, in light of the increasing pressures of markets and society (Higgins *et al.*, 2014; van Bommel, 2014 Milne and Gray, 2013). Others have described IR as a temporarily fad and fashion practice adopted by companies for legitimacy purposes (Brown and Dillard, 2014; Zappettini and Unerman, 2016; Flower, 2015; Thomson, 2014).

According to Higgins *et al.* (2014), the narratives on sustainability produced by integrated reports are often deployed in relation to organisational perspectives and shareholder driven purposes. Moreover, the persuasive (i.e. rhetorical) "story-telling" of integrated reporting on sustainability, make it a fascinating practice that is increasingly adopted by private and public organizations to meet strategic drivers and institutional expectations as opposed to social and environmental issues (Higgins *et al.* 2014).

---

[2] Building on Abrahamson and Baumard (2008), Cho *et al.*, 2015 define an organisational façade as a symbolic front erected by organisational participants to hide negative performance and reassure their organisational stakeholders of the legitimacy of the organisation and its management. (Cho *et al.*, 2015 p. 82).

Also, Zappettini and Unerman (2016) maintain that IR refers to sustainability as a discourse often constructed around internal organization speculations more than external and holistic discursive orientations. They suggest that, by adopting IR, organisations primarily represent themselves as "being or becoming (financially, economically and commercially) sustainable" and focusing merely on certain actions or decisions that would safeguard the interest of a broader number of shareholders as sustainable, thus reconsidering sustainability issues looking first at the long-term growth and profitability (Zappettini and Unerman, 2016 p. 538). In particular, they maintain that organizations adopt IR as a legitimacy tool to rhetorically validate their activities as sustainable and defining sustainability or sustainable development as a concept that is "frequently mixed with and embedded in and bent towards financial and macro-economic propositions to suit specific organisational narratives and communicative purposes" (Zappettini and Unerman, 2016 p. 538).

In this regard, van Bommel (2014) maintains that integrated reporting fails to find a "legitimate" compromise (or integration) between sustainability and financial issues, and among multiple interests, maintaining ambiguity on sustainability instead of reducing it (van Bommel, 2014, p. 1160).

These factors have increased the scepticism of many academics regarding the reliability of the information provided by sustainability, corporate responsibility reports, and most recently integrated report, which have been labelled to be "partial and mostly, fairly trivial" (Gray, 2006a; O'Dwyer *et al.*, 2011). In particular, some studies have emphasised the need for mandated and externally verified sustainability reporting within different sectors (see, e.g., O'Dwyer, Unerman and Hession, 2005; Adams, 2004) and have called for greater sustainability assurance within organisations (O'Dwyer and Owen, 2005; Gond *et al.*, 2009).

Adams (2004) assessed the potential of standards and guidelines for sustainability reporting to reduce what she calls the "reporting-performance" portrayal gap and thus improve corporate accountability. She concluded that additional measures, reporting guidelines, better audit guidelines, mandatory audit requirements and better governance systems are needed. Along these lines, O'Dwyer *et al.* (2011) suggested possible ways for understanding sustainability assurance in searching for credibility and reliability of reporting contents. However, as illustrated in Chapter two, although many institutions have attempted to provide guidelines and standards for regulating sustainability reporting, there is still evidence of a mismatch between what an organisation says and what it does to be sustainable (Higgins *et al.*, 2014).

Considering the contradicting definitions and positions attributable to sustainability and organisations' attempts to represent and define what sustainability means within their reports, some researchers have concluded that there is "clearly no single 'sustainability' that can be known and accounted for" (Gray, 2010 p. 56). Thus, what sustainability means within organisations is, according to Gray (2010), an exercise of imagination, which necessitates a continuous collection of information, actions, informed decisions and measurement of the environmental, social and economic aspects of an organisation.

Consistent with this perspective, a number of authors have argued that accounting practices in general provide a limited understanding of the complexity of organisational life (see also Chapman, 1997; Lillis, 2002), and have suggested that the possibility for accounting to be objective and to represent certain aspects of an organisation in a true manner is difficult to achieve (Roberts and Scapens, 1985).

Historically, accounting systems aimed at providing unambiguous and uncontested sets of organisational objectives, encouraging a numerical picture of reality (Roberts and Scapens, 1985). Since 1947, when the UK Companies Act proposed the idea of presenting a "true and fair view", accounting has been grounded in a quest for "objective" representation (Bayou *et al.* 2011). Many financial statements use 'truth' or its synonyms to describe a desired quality for accounting reports. That is, accounting and reporting, as forms of internal and external representation, aim to provide something factual, something able to represent reality as it is (Bayou *et al.* 2011). According to Solomons (1991), accounting data are "complete", since they can faithfully represent the underlying economic reality and bring together all relevant interests of members in a community (Solomons, 1991). Therefore, accounting practices have often been described as a mirror through which an organisation represents itself (Roberts and Scapens, 1985).

However, the literature has raised questions about the capability of accounting and reporting practices to faithfully represent how organisations operate (see for example, Hines, 1988; Morgan, 1988; Shapiro, 1997; Mattessich, 2003; Messner, 2009; Jordan and Messner; 2012). Moreover, Shapiro (1997) recognizes that neither accounting nor any other scientific method provides faithful representations of the activities performed within an organisation. According to Shapiro (1997), there are two arguments against the representational faithfulness of accounting information. The first maintains that representational faithfulness should be rejected because "no set of financial statements can completely represent all features of reality or completely satisfy the information needs of all possible financial statement users" (Shapiro, 1997, p. 172). The second refers to the degree of representational faithfulness of accounting and financial statements, which is not easily measurable and is biased by people's beliefs, attitudes and opinions about the most appropriate ways of representing an organisation's internal and external reality (Shapiro, 1997, p. 172).

Accordingly, Mattessich (2003) maintains that accounting, as a form of communication, is poorly equipped for representing an organisation's operations with any degree of precision. He maintains that accounting, like a portrait, always provides an imperfect representation of. what it aims to represent (Mattessich, 2003).

For example, by taking a look at the lithograph by Escher known as *The Hand with Reflecting Globe*,[3] Morgan (1988) focuses on the problems that accounting has in representing reality by arguing that it can provide just partial and incomplete representations of what it aims to represent. In particular, he affirms that:

> "[accounts] are always engaged in interpreting a complex reality, partially, and in a way that is heavily weighted in favour of what the accountant is able to measure and chooses to measure, through the particular scheme of accounting to be adopted" (Morgan, 1988, p. 480 – see also Gray, 2010, p. 49).

Consequently, accountants (and more generally managers), like artists, grasp and articulate complex realities in partial ways, and this grasping helps sustain the realities as being perceived and the definitions as being understood in multiple ways that are not necessarily coherent (Morgan, 1988).

The partial representations provided by accounting and reporting practices have also effects on the accountability of organizations actions and performances. Accordingly, Butler (2005) sees accounting as a type of narrative of the self that is intrinsically limited to what the self can recount and "depends upon (its) ability to relay a set of sequential events with plausible transitions" (Butler, 2005, p. 12).

Building on Butler (2005), Messner (2009) argues that organisations' ability to represent and account for their own actions (accountability) is subject to three main limitations, which indicate that any account is imperfect in relation to its ability to ground organisations' responsibility. Messner (2009) identified three limits of organisations' accountability: *Opacity, Exposition and Mediation*. First, accounting is *opaque*, since it is unable to fully record (e.g. to account) and report (e.g. to recount) the situations in which organisations are involved. Accounting is not able to fully justify

[3] Escher's lithograph, *the Hand With Reflecting Globe*, depicts the artist hand holding a reflective sphere. In the reflection, the viewer is bound into the picture as if he or she were standing in Escher's shoes.

managers' decisions and judgments, as these may go beyond the realm of the calculable. Second, organisations are *exposed* to the judgements and prescriptions of external stakeholders, regulators, interpreters and observers. Such judgements are not necessarily passive but contribute to constitute and define the organisation. Third, organisations' accounting is *mediated* by a set of social norms that structure the scene it aims to address.

In other words, one cannot expect organisations to provide an objective account of themselves because the account portrayed may be biased by the interests of senior management or certain shareholders/stakeholders to the detriment of others (Roberts and Scapens, 1985).

Most of the literature mentioned above concentrates on the practices for representing, reporting, and accounting for organizational aspects and initiatives. However, these studies have not specifically addressed the complex relationship between accounting's incompleteness (i.e. as it inevitably fails to provide a full representation of organizational reality), as well as the inherent ambiguity of the issues that accounting practices attempts to represent. In particular, studies on accounting and reporting representations of sustainability, focused on the need for reducing the gap between what companies actually *do* and what they *say* about sustainability. However, this gap does not necessarily have distortive effects.

Some recent studies show that accounting plays a more fundamental role than the accounting-as-mirror literature suggests. These studies argue that accounting and reporting practices constitute economic and organisational reality as much as they attempt to represent it (Hines, 1988). As emphasised by Ahrens and Chapman (2007), accounting cannot be understood simply in relation to its representational approach, but it plays a fundamental role in shaping organisational context, necessitating interaction and stimulating actions among different managers and perspectives (Ahrens and Chapman, 2007).

Jordan and Messner (2012) suggest that the "problem of incompleteness" of accounting is not a function of the representational qualities of the information provided per se, but rather depends on how this information relates to the world of action. They argue that this is not an ontological, but a methodological problem (Jordan and Messner, 2012). Thus, according to Andon *et al.* (2007) accounting incompleteness can be addressed by attempting to "repair" accounting practices bridging the gap left between reality and representation and exploring their role in sustaining and shaping organisational activity.

Accordingly, the sceptical view of accounting and reporting for sustainability is nurtured by a lack of research into the intra-organisational outcomes of devoting attention to sustainability (Bebbington, 2007; Milne and

Grubnic, 2011), and also by the scant attention devoted to the role of accounting and reporting practices for influencing actions in relation to sustainability within organisations (Durden, 2008; Herzig *et al.* 2012). While acknowledging the gap between what organizations *say* and what they actually *do* about sustainability, such literature does not address the role that the processes of designing accounting and reporting practices may play in influencing organisations to embrace sustainability as a strategic goal in order to address social and environmental responsibilities (Gond *et al.*, 2012; Henri and Journeault, 2010).

The following paragraph explores how accounting and reporting practices have effects beyond the representations they aim to provide.

3.3. The role of accounting and reporting practices in constructing organisational concepts

In contrast to the criticism of accounting and reporting highlighted in this chapter, one of the most useful characteristics of accounting is its aggregation properties and its role as a common language among managers with different backgrounds, experiences and knowledge (Busco and Quattrone, 2015; Hall, 2010). As a form of textual and verbal communication, accounting and reporting practices allow managers to tailor information to specific operational concerns and provide a context for debate and discussion of the meanings and implications of the information provided (Hall, 2010).

The inherent incompleteness of accounting and reporting practices contributes to stimulate managers' involvement in their preparation, questioning and debate about the most suitable performance to communicate, with the intention of giving meaning to certain organisational phenomena (Messner, 2009). In this regard, Ahrens and Chapman (2007) maintain that through such functions, accounting can potentially make a significant contribution to the ways in which organisational motivations take place and how multiple intentions are coordinated (Ahrens and Chapman, 2007, p. 310 emphasis added).

This indicates that the relevance of accounting information does not necessarily depend on its ability to depict operational processes accurately or completely, but on its function as a medium through which diverse operational considerations are rendered communicable through a common language. In this way, accounting and reporting practices can function as a medium for facilitating communication among managers with different information requirements, background and functional experience to better understand certain aspects of organization reality instead of representing them faithfully (Ahrens, 1997; Briers and Chua, 2001; Andon *et al.*, 2007; Quattrone, 2009; Hall, 2010).

Briars and Chua (2001) argue that valuable accounting representations are not simply those that have a high degree of representational faithfulness. Instead, building on Latour (1987), Briars and Chua (2001) illustrate that certain accounting practices are not adopted because they are perceived as giving the right answers for specific situations, but because their usability makes people discuss the credibility, practicality and consistency of these practices and the information reported.

Quattrone (2009) argues that accounting practices are useful, not because they guide users within certain institutionalized and prescriptive guidelines, but rather because they contribute to organizing knowledge. Likewise, Ahrens and Chapman (2007) maintain that accounting cannot be understood simply in relation to its representational approach, but it instead plays a fundamental role in shaping the context by involving and stimulating actions among different participants and perspectives.

Andon *et al.* (2007) illustrates that the implementation of a Balanced Scorecard for an Australian telecommunications organisation engaged managers in ongoing experimentation and discussion about the appropriateness and applicability of the measures used (p. 293). Furthermore, Wouters and Wilderom (2008) illustrate how accounting practices make users aware of the rationale behind certain management control mechanisms and enable them to act on it. They propose that the involvement of managers in the development of a performance measurement system contributes to the enhancement of its management control nature, while it contributes to the improvement of experienced-based knowledge allowing experimentation as well as raising employees' professionalism.

Similarly, Revellino and Mouritsen (2009) explored the case study of the development of a traffic control system in a listed Italian organisation in order to illustrate how management control systems (MCS) provide a space in which ongoing innovation activities may be tried and tested. Moreover, Jørgensen and Messner (2010), demonstrate how managers and engineers draw upon various informal arrangements in order to learn what is going on in their organization. They show how engineers who were working on new product development, evaluate different design alternatives based on accounting information and a set of strategic objectives that cannot be easily translated into accounting numbers, aiming to get a wider view of the organisation's activity.

In organisational settings, with multiple and potentially competing intentions, accounting is used to engage different perspectives and members in the production of accounts that are based on compromise, temporary agreement and continuous adjustment (Chenhall, 2013; Busco and Quattrone, 2015). Some researchers have demonstrated that situations where managers share transparent information and reach agreement are the exception, rather than the rule (Cohen, *et al.* 1972; Cooper, 1981).

Thus, accounting practices engage users not because they provide readymade answers to pre-established questions about administrative problems, but because they create a space, in which users question and practice accounting information (Busco and Quattrone, 2015; Quattrone, 2009; 2015).

In this regard, Busco and Quattrone (2015) theorize that accounting practices, such as the Balanced Scorecard (BSC), function as rhetorical "machines"[4] (See Bolzoni, 1995; and Carruthers, 1990). According to Busco and Quattrone (2015), rhetorical machines were not used to persuade other "auditors" regarding the veracity of certain facts but were used as valid instruments (i.e. visual schemas, graphs, tables) for logically structuring and organizing the content of orators'speeches and for mnemonically crafting the relations between multiple definitions, texts, discourses and images (see Carruthers 1998), which are discussed on the spot. Actually, rhetorical machines

> "had a crucial spatial connotation as they helped knowledge classification and invention through the use of visual and spatially based schemas, and allowed 're-presentations' designed for being open to interpretation, appropriation and translation, beyond any stable and ultimate form of objective and univocal truth" (Busco and Quattrone, 2015, p. 1240).

Consequently, accounting practices operate as platforms wherein "knowledge" is continuously classified and questioned, the different interests are accommodated through regular processes of interrogation and reinvention, and engagement is sustained through participation in a series of recurrent activities (Busco and Quattrone, 2015). In their framework, the BSC provides a common space in which knowledge of strategies, objectives and activities are created, not by providing answers to its users (e.g. by providing numerical performance measures that completely explain the

---

[4] As noted by Carruthers (1998), in rhetoric the Latin term *machina* is not synonymous with 'mechanical'and 'predictable movements', as it is now interpreted, rather it addresses anything that helps in the construction of something, be this a building or, indeed, thinking (Carruthers, 1998). In rhetoric, the term *machina* then referred to any instrument useful for building and edifying thoughts through meditation (Busco and Quattrone, 2015).

trade-off between initiatives and/or objectives), but rather by stimulating questions that continuously produce possibilities for constructing new knowledge and understanding, while mediating amongst various users at different organisational levels.

Hence, accounting and reporting create a space for engagement by enabling questions to emerge from the information provided and, at the same time, debate these questions by challenging the sources that generated them (Chenhall, 2013).

This process of questioning and interrogation is generated by the necessity to provide a complete representation of an organisation's activities within a unitary system of performance measurement and to satisfy the expectations of the organisation's functions, divisions, individual managers, as well as those of the stakeholders (Wouters and Roijmans, 2011). The frictions and the overlap of multiple performance criteria and intentions generate productive re-combinations of knowledge by sustaining a pragmatic organisational reflexivity (Stark, 2009, p. 27). In this way, a "resourceful dissonance" is produced that can enable organisations to benefit from this process of debate. Such dissonance is intrinsically productive, because it requires managers to overcome accounting incompleteness to better understand certain organisational issues (Stark, 2009). The next section considers this further, in light of efforts to provide accounts of organisational performance in relation to sustainability.

3.4. The role of accounting and reporting in fostering sustainability within organisations

Recent studies illustrate the constitutive role of business accounting and reporting representations for sustainable development (Milne *et al.*, 2009; Christensen *et al.* 2013; 2015). For example, Milne *et al.* (2009) argues that, by enabling or constraining actions, an organisation can attempt to represent its sustainability initiatives as strongly implicated in the way in which an organisation has come to 'know' and 'do' sustainability. Also, Christensen *et al.* (2015) highlight how communications about sustainability,

> "cannot – and should not – be a perfect reflection of existing organisational sustainability practices. Although differences between words and actions in the sustainability arena are usually disdained, ...such differences have the potential to move the field forward toward higher ideals and superior practices" (pp. 139-140).

In this regard, the development of sustainability reporting not only changes the organisation's culture, but in some ways also changes organisational processes and practices (Adams and McNicholas, 2007).

Some studies have investigated the role of social and environmental accounting and reporting practices in stimulating organisational change in relation to sustainable development (see for example Adams and Mc Nicholas, 2007; Contrafatto 2013; 2014; Spence and Rinaldi, 2014).

Adams and McNicholas (2007) used an action research case study to illustrate how sustainability reporting was adopted to embed sustainability principles as part of the organisational culture. They found that sustainability reporting operates as a relevant "means of introducing and reinforcing sustainability principles throughout the organisation by improving their integration into planning and decision making, leading to improvements in sustainability performance" (p. 398). In contrast to O'Dwyer (2002), Adams and McNicholas (2007) demonstrate that sustainability reporting operates as a management learning process for the preparation of the corporate report.

Accordingly, Contrafatto and Burns (2013) focus on the role of Social Environmental Accounting and Reporting (SEAR) practices in fostering organisational change, as well as the role of management accounting in fostering progress towards sustainable development. They conducted a longitudinal case study to show how dominant business imperatives and the profit-oriented ways of operating in the context of "business as usual", could have limited organisations' possibility to "embed" sustainability issues within their routine activities. Although, their findings highlight complexity in the development and effects of SEAR practice over time and illustrate the potential limits of this development within a profit-seeking organisation, they also recognise that SEAR practices have the potential to integrate sustainability principles and values into organisational strategies. Furthermore, Contrafatto (2014) explored the process through which social and environmental accounting and reporting (SEAR) become widely accepted and taken for granted categories within organisations, supporting the construction of shared meanings around the notion of social and environmental responsibility.

In a similar vein, Spence and Rinaldi (2014) demonstrated how corporate engagement with sustainability reporting can be enacted, maintained and transformed in practice, due to the central role played by accounting practices in such processes. Their main contribution emerges from the examination of the conditions under which business practices engage with sustainability. Using a governmentality lens, they refer to sustainability as "a regime of practice", which is enacted, maintained and transformed to share a common approach to sustainability across the organisational boundaries of the supply chain (p. 449).

In contrast to conventional thinking, accounting and reporting practices for sustainability can encourage an organisation to move toward sustainability improvements (Christensen *et al.*, 2015a, pp. 139-140). In particular, Christensen *et al.* (2013) maintains that the ways in which organisations talk about their activities and performance on sustainability cannot be considered as being separate from the actions they take, since they are constitutive of organisational life. Citing Austin (1962), Christensen *et al.* (2013) affirms that organisational accounts and reports are not merely descriptions, but prescriptions[5] with "performative" facets that provoke specific actions. In their view:

> "Even when corporate ambitions to do good vis-à-vis society do not reflect managerial action, talk about such ambitions provides articulation of ideals, beliefs, values and frameworks for decisions – in other words, raw material for (re)constructing the organisations" (p. 376).

According to Christensen *et al.* (2013), accounting representations and discussions about sustainability represent actions themselves and serve as *aspirational* disclosures and constitutive devices through which organisations pursue and define sustainability (Christensen *et al.,* 2013). In particular, Christensen *et al.* (2013) emphasises that organisational statements and talks about sustainability are not just descriptions, but entails an aspiration, which ultimately affect organizing. In this regard, accounting and reporting practices may produce sustainability aspirations that do not unfold automatically or predictably into corporate reporting initiatives, but they can "help to define or illuminate a collective 'horizon' of excellence to which employees, NGOs and other stakeholders can hold the organisation accountable" (Christensen *et al.* 2015b, p. 21).

Along these lines, Cho *et al.* (2015) build on prior studies on organized hypocrisy and organizational façade to explore the discrepancies between corporation's talks, decisions and actions, and emphasise the enabling effects of these discrepancies. They argue that organizational façades and organized hypocrisy may enable greater flexibility in managing stakeholders' expectations and provide opportunities for action through the aspirations that they entail. Following Brunsson (2007), they argue that in many cir-

---

[5] The etymology of the word prescription come from Latin *praescriptionem* (nominative praescriptio) "a writing before, order, direction", a noun of action from the past participle stem of praescribere, "write before, prefix in writing; ordain, determine in advance", from prae "before" (see pre-) + scribere "to write" (see script).

cumstances talks and decisions are held to be inconsistent with actions. This means that companies are likely to articulate their talks specifically around their weak areas, relying upon the inconsistency between talks and present (unsatisfactory) actions as a way to close the time distance from future (and more satisfactory) actions. To this end, talks need to be 'aspirational', motivating organizations to strive for a better future (Cho *et al.*, 2015, p. 84; see also Christensen *et al.*, 2013).

This point is further expanded by Gibassier *et al.* (2017) in relation to integrated reporting. By drawing on the work on accounting innovations by Busco and Quattrone (2015), Gibassier *et al.* (2017) argued that such innovations as integrated reporting stimulate action through the promises held by their mythical dimension, even if these promises are never fulfilled. In this sense, integrated reporting is 'aspirational' as it praises an imaginary future which stimulates more tailored accounting practices. From this point of view, accounting and reporting practices perform a social function beyond their mere representational ability.

However, for this to happen, it is necessary that many different voices continuously participate in the articulation of sustainability in the context of their organisations' ideals and values. "And while such plurality of voices may produce confusion and inconsistency, tolerance towards inconsistencies in the talk and behaviour of organisations allow them to expand and explore their capabilities within the realm of sustainability" (Christensen *et al.* 2013, p. 386).

Guthey and Morsing (2014) propose that any organisation's statement about sustainability cannot be treated as a clear or consistent agenda, or even as a unified coalition or movement toward collective action, but rather as a "forum" were different opinions regarding corporate activity towards sustainability are debated (Guthey and Morsing, 2014). In this perspective, accounting for sustainability cannot represent a fixed set of directions that define and describe, sometimes in minute detail, how managers and employees are supposed to think and act in specific situations. Rather, it should be understood to be a set of guiding values that continuously evolves through the input and the challenges from managers, employees, and citizens.

In this sense, organisations' accounting and reporting practices cannot be judged solely by the partial representations that they produce, since the process entails actions, aspirations and intentions of the individuals involved (Busco and Quattrone, 2015).

In this regard, the "open ended" nature of the concept of sustainability, and the multiple interpretations that this concept entails, as well as the incapacity of accounting and reporting practices to provide complete representation of organizations activities towards sustainability, offer an opportunity to 'talk about it' in several ways, thereby, providing the potential to stimulate debate among different perspectives.

Most research on accounting and reporting for sustainability focuses on the necessity to provide a complete representation of sustainability through accounting reports (Spence, 2007; Tregidga *et al.*, 2014; Milne and Gray, 2013), and also on suppressing conflict between financial and non-financial performance. The ongoing attempt to give meaning to and represent sustainability within organisations has allowed multiple 'discourses'about sustainability – i.e. different ways of talking about, understanding and interpreting its contents – to unfold. These discourses have both a reflective and a constructive power within organisations.

Therefore, further research is needed into how organisations represent their goals and aspirations about sustainability as an integral part of their reporting process. In particular, this research explores the potentially enabling processes that multiple understandings of sustainability and accounting incompleteness stimulate. This research adds to the studies reviewed above by exploring how discourses on sustainability are produced in practice within organisations. Further, the role of (and implications for) accounting and reporting practices within this process has been explored.

3.5. Identifying gaps and situating the research objectives

By relying upon these studies, this research maintains that the ambiguity of sustainability as a concept, and the impossibility to fully capture it through accounting and reporting practices, do not mean that any attempt to represent it inevitably leads to distortion or obfuscates 'reality'. Rather, the way in which this concept is presented through accounting and reporting practices can have a constructive effect on organization through the aspirations that their production entails. Also, the "open ended" nature of the concept of sustainability offers the opportunity to 'talk about it' in several ways, thereby having the potential to stimulate change.

From this perspective, accounting and reporting practices for sustainability cannot represent a fixed set of directions that define and describe, sometimes in minute detail, how organizations act in relation to sustainability. Rather, they can be understood as being a set of practices that continuously evolve through input and challenges from managers, employees, and possibly other stakeholders.

Tregidga *et al.* (2012) suggest that more research is needed to understand the factors and motives underpinning the production of the organisational message of sustainability. In particular, they suggest that socio-historical analyses are needed, which explicitly theorize the production of organisational messages using interpretive and qualitative perspectives and methods (Tregidga *et al.* 2012). They call for studies analysing the construction of the message, looking at the instances used and adopted when deciding on 'what is to be said' and 'how it is to be said', focusing the attention to specific language features (e.g. metaphors) and examples of text (Tregidga *et al.* 2012).

Tregidga *et al.* (2012), argue that "more studies analysing the notions of meaning, quality and accountability in organisational reporting and communication are needed because an examination of how organisational reporting and communication is constructed and its potential consequences (both intended and unintended) remains underdeveloped" (p. 228).

Following this stream of research, the aim of this study is twofold. First, this study aims *to explore the role of accounting and reporting practices, and in particular integrated reporting, as organizations attempt to represent sustainability.*

This study explores how organizations' attempts to represent sustainability (i.e. its represent*ing* – the process of representation) affect the way in which organizations understand and report about sustainability, changing its meaning over time.

In particular, this study explores whether and how accounting and reporting practices provide the conditions for the concept of sustainability to be filled with meanings, and how these meanings unfold, eventually leading to evolving accounting and reporting practices.

Considering the need to understand the aspirations and motives underpinning the way in which organizations construct their message of sustainability and with the aim to achieve the research objective above mentioned, this study relies on the analysis of the reports published by DAPHNE, a multinational company that operates in the oil and gas sector.

Through the case of DAPHNE, this study analyses the evolution of DAPHNE's sustainability approach and reporting process from 1996 (when the company's first Health, Safety and Environmental report was published) to 2015. DAPHNE's reporting evolution has been analysed distinguishing three main phases (from 1996 to 2005; from 2006 to 2009; from 2010 to 2015). For each phase, the key practices and dynamics through which the meaning of sustainability emerged and evolved within DAPHNE have been analysed, together with the different types of reports published over the years. In particular, the research illustrates the main external contingencies that influenced the adoption of the reports, the meaning of sustainability associated with them, the key practices used and the units responsible for the preparation of the report.

The following chapter explains the theoretical lens adopted in this research.

3.6. Summary and some further thoughts

The studies reviewed in this chapter emphasize the central role that accounting and reporting practices play in the ongoing attempt to give meaning to sustainability issues within organisational strategies and initiatives. However, these studies have mainly concentrated on the truthfulness or reliability of sustainability reports, without delving into the practices that produce such representations, as well as the actions taken by the actors involved in the reporting process.

The first part of this chapter included a review on the inadequacy and incompleteness of accounting and reporting when attempting to represent sustainability as an organisation's strategic objective (see Sections 3.1, 3.2). Although organisations engage with sustainability issues to pursue win-win solutions, accounting and reporting practices have the potential to stimulate innovation, motivating organisations and their members to develop and stimulate further actions towards sustainable development (Christensen *et al.*, 2013) (see Sections 3.3 and 3.4).

Building on this literature, this study maintains that it is necessary to understand whether and how these representations, (and the aspirations that they entail), are leveraged by managers in an attempt to make sustainability meaningful within organisations, rather than trying to reduce the gap between accounting representations and the reality within an organisation. Sustainability's definitional gaps and accounting's inability to provide complete and faithful representations of an organisation's sustainability approach both offer a possibility for further definitions to emerge and unfold. In this sense, accounting and reporting are relevant not because they provide unequivocal definitions of sustainability (Gray, 2010; Tregidga *et al.* 2014), but because they provide a space in which multiple definitions unfold and emerge in practice.

Chapter 4
A THEORETICAL FRAME: DISCOURSE WITHIN ORGANIZATIONS

4.1. Analysing text and defining organizations' discourse

Discourse is defined as "a particular way of talking about and understanding the world (or an aspect of the world)" (Jorgensen and Phillips, 2002, p. 1). These understandings, however, are not aimed at representing an aspect of the world as it is but have a fundamental role in constructing social understandings of reality (Berger and Luckmann, 1967).

This definition of discourse has been influenced by the work of Foucault who defines discourse as "a practice [...] of signifying the world, constituting and constructing the world in meaning" (Fairclough, 1992, p. 64). Foucault maintains that discourse influences the way in which a certain aspect of the world can be meaningfully talked and reasoned about (Foucault, 1979, p. 49). Therefore, objects of conversation such as "madness"; "freedom"; "literacy"; or even "progress"; "nature"; or in this case "sustainability", do not exist in reality since they only become meaningful through discourse (See Fairclough, 1992, pp. 41-43). Thus, social reality is, to a certain sense, produced and made real through discourses and social interactions that cannot be fully understood without reference to the discourses that give them meaning (Fairclough, 1992; Foucault, 1972, 1977, 1980; Hajer, 1995; Phillips and Hardy, 2002).

Accordingly, a large part of the literature on organizational discourse examines the ways in which discourses are created within organizations (Phillips and Hardy, 2002; Fairhurst and Putnam, 2004). More specifically, organizational discourses are represented as oral, written and symbolic media, which are used to "describe, represent, interpret and theorise what we take to be the facticity of organizational life" (Oswick *et al.*, 2000, p. 1116). These verbal and written media have the potential to "bring organizationally related objects into being" (Jorgensen and Phillips, 2002, p. 9) by producing, disseminating and carrying out collections of practices through communication tools of different forms, e.g. email, meetings, reports, documents (Fairhurst and Cooren, 2004; Grant *et al.*, 2004; Hardy *et al.*, 2005; Jorgensen and Phillips, 2002). These practices result from continuous reciprocal arrangements (e.g. conversations, narratives and texts) among organizational actors, which do not simply reflect an organizational reality but contribute to constructing it, by facilitating organizing processes and improving communication (Hardy *et al.*, 2000; Oswick, 2000; Hardy *et al.*, 2005).

For example, narratives and stories play a fundamental role in the co-construction of verbal and written interactions among actors who are narrating a certain "account" (be it true or fictional) and sustaining the interest of a specific group (Grant *et al.*, 2004, p. 5). Also, narratives operate as instruments for the collection of past, present and forecastable events through which individuals explain a social phenomenon (Czarniawska, 1998, p. 2).

Texts are produced through sequenced discursive acts and as part of the same conversation (Fairclough, 1992). If conversation represents the dynamics of organizing, then texts represent the "surface" from which an organization is read. Conversations construct texts, which in turn become suitable sites for future conversations (Taylor and Robichaud, 2004). Texts represent "the done" and the "material" confirmation of discourse (Taylor and Van Every, 2000). Texts represent the main medium for knowing and communicating within organizations. They are co-constructed and function ideologically to represent the interests of certain groups of stakeholders (Boje, 1995; Czarniawska, 1997, 1998; Mumby, 1987).

Text, as a form of narrative, operate as a sense-making device and may have important implications on organizing processes and practices. In particular, texts play a fundamental role in developing relations and systems of interaction among multiple actors, who are involved in the production of written documents or graphical devices (Putnam and Cooren, 2004). Such interactions are not so much the result of disconnected utterances; instead, they are produced through ongoing linguistic exchanges among actors who draw on a broader discourse. Conversely, discourses function as resources for interaction and for further conversations (Fairclough, 1992).

By exploring texts as *sites* where organizing occurs, Taylor and Robichaud (2004) consider them to be practices through which organizational members co-orient their understandings towards a shared object of concern. However, texts and conversations do not dissolve or compensate for differences. Instead, they give manifestation to discussions between diverse and competing interests (Taylor and Robichaud, 2004). [1]

[1] From latin *dis (two) – currere (to move to)*, which means running from one side to

In this sense, organizational discourses are made up of a multitude of practices, such as linguistic discourse, symbols or narratives that do not simply reflect an organizational reality, but rather, construct it (Oswick *et al.*, 2000, p. 1116). The following section introduces the main studies on organizational discourse, exploring how written and oral discourses influence an organization's social reality.

4.2. Approaches to organizational discourse analysis

As described in the previous section, organizing emerges through discourse and discursive practices, (e.g. text and conversations), which operate as mediums through which group members' intentions compromise and act in order to give meaning to a certain organizational aspect (Phillips and Hardy, 2002). This interpretation of organizational discourse has influenced prior research on "discourse analysis", which has been classified according to certain theoretical and methodological approaches.

Some studies on discourse have relied on Foucault's work and emphasise the constitutive, and not merely reflective, role of discourse (see Foucault, 1972). For example, according to Fairclough (1992, p. 64), language not only represents the world but also signifies it, by 'constituting and constructing' meaning within it. Likewise, Phillips and Hardy (2002) emphasise both the constitutive role of discourses, as well as the importance of understanding the context in which discourses are produced and the social practices involved in such production (see, also, Fairclough, 1992).

According to Alvesson and Kärreman (2000), "discourse analysis" refers to the analysis of specific texts and to the relationship between discourses and social orders. Alvesson and Kärreman (2000) distinguish between two different approaches to discourse analysis. The first approach considers *discourses* as structured in talk and texts through which different actors engage in social interactions. This approach emphasises the fact that *discourses* are created and changed in everyday discursive practices. It requires a more systematic analysis of organizations' spoken and written text in order to determine how they are produced and how they create interaction among multiple perspectives within organizations. It considers *discourses* at the local level of analysis, focusing on how talk and written texts are practiced, thus creating knowledge and giving meaning to certain aspects of reality. At the local level, the analysis of discourse focuses on the use or the

---

another and at least between two sides. In this case, it is interpreted as exchanging ideas and thoughts from one side to another.

exchange of certain metaphors, rhetoric, and utterances through which conversations and texts are produced (Fairhurst and Putnam, 2004).

The second approach refers to *Discourses* as being the general production and generation of ideas in a historically situated time (p. 8).[2] In this regard, *Discourses* are defined as being both contextual and the broader systems of thought through which the formation and articulation of ideas and texts take place during a certain period (Alvesson and Kärreman, 2000; Fairhurst and Putnam, 2004). This approach defines *Discourses* at the macro level as the general and prevalent systems that influence the generation and articulation of ideas in a certain period of time and social space (Alvesson and Kärreman, 2000; Fairhurst and Putnam, 2004; Jorgensen and Phillips, 2002). Studies that focus on *Discourses* at the macro level are considered to be "context sensitive" studies. These studies offer interesting insights into cross-cultural communication, demonstrating how subjects' cultural and social backgrounds are highly implicated in the construction of social discourse (Schiffrin, 1994). Some studies, for instance, have placed emphasis on how institutional context informs and shapes language and discourse, and also affects the way in which individuals perform and pursue their respective organizational tasks and goals (Drew and Sorjonen, 1997).

To better understand the different theoretical approaches that take place in discourse analysis, Phillips and Hardy (2002) provide a useful tool that combines the theoretical approach proposed by Alvesson and Kärreman (2000) with other studies that consider discourses as being shaped by systems of power relations, ideology and domination (critical studies), as well as with constructivist studies that consider discourses as being a social construction that constitutes social reality.

Constructivist studies regard discourses as builders of the organizing process within organizations (Berger and Luckmann, 1967; Fairhurst and Putnam, 2004; Mumby, 2004; Oswick; 2000). Through discourse, organizational members interact, co-construct and co-constitute different aspects of an organization. According to Marshak and Grant (2008), constructivist studies place discourses at the centre of sense-making and of the ongoing social construction of reality. However, the production of texts and narratives can generate competing interpretations, rather than an objective description of reality (Marshak and Grant, 2008).

Critical studies regarding organizational discourse focus on the ways in which contending constituencies and players use power and political relations to privilege and affirm discourses that give advantage to their interests

[2] In this case, Alvesson and Kärreman, (2000) use an uppercase "D" to distinguish the two definitions of discourse.

over others (Fairclough, 1992; Fairclough and Wodak, 1997; Hardy *et al.* 2000; 2004; Phillips and Hardy, 1997; Phillips and Hardy, 2002; Wodak and Meyer, 2009). Critical studies consider discourses as sites in which multiple interests and intentions match and struggle to give meaning to a certain organizational reality in ways that serve their interests (Mumby, 2004; Marshak and Grant, 2008). Systems of competing interests and power relations, however, are not fixed in time and space (Hardy and Thomas, 2015), and change according to an organization's consciousness, mind-sets and social agreements, which require challenging or changing the prevailing texts and understandings that are endorsed by those presently and/or historically in power (Marshak and Grant, 2008). The ways in which power and competing relations shape discourse are a central concern of critical studies in organizational discourse (Marshak and Grant, 2008).

To facilitate the comprehension of different research studies and approaches to organizational discourse analysis, Phillips and Hardy (2002) represent them in the following graph (See Figure 4.1).

Figure 4.1 – Different approaches to discourse analysis (Phillips and Hardy, 2002; p. 20).

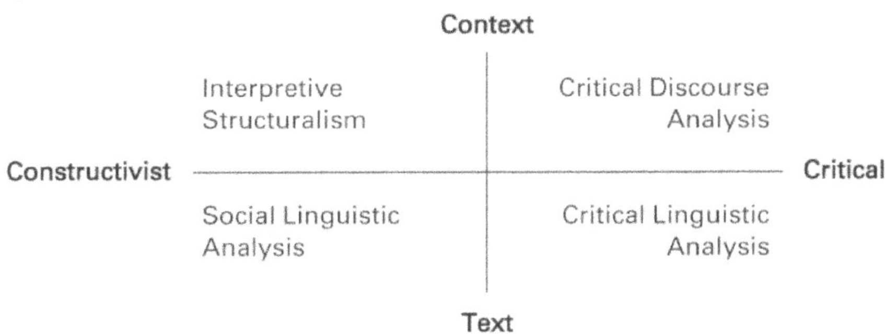

The horizontal axis of Figure 4.1 places the constructivist research on the left side and critical studies on discourse analysis on the right side. Then the vertical axis distinguishes between contextual-oriented studies versus more textual-analytical studies. However, constructivist and critical positions are not meant to be static, since they may be interrelated. A significant number of studies embrace either, or both, a social constructivist and/or a critical perspective approach (Hardy *et al.* 2000). Some analyse the impact of languages and other discursive vehicles, such as texts, in transforming social reality by exploring how these vehicles influence members' behaviours, mind-sets and intentions (Hardy *et al.* 2000; Phillips and Hardy, 2002).

By combining the two axes, Phillips and Hardy (2002) identify four major, theoretical approaches in discourse analysis such as *Social-linguistic*

Analysis; *Interpretive Structuralism*; *Critical Discourse Analysis*; and *Critical-linguistic Analysis*.

Social-linguistic Analysis is constructivist and text-based. This research approach aims to take a close look at the structure and content of texts in order to explore organizations and the construction of their reality. The social-linguistic approach focuses on the analysis of interviews (e.g., Dunford and Jones, 2000), participant observations (Hardy, Lawrence, and Phillips, 1998), focus groups (Beech, 2000), and stories to understand what role texts may play in organizing and constructing a certain organizational phenomenon. A significant amount of social linguistic research examines oral and written texts, such as recordings of conversations in detail (Mauws, 2000). However, this approach pays little attention to the contexts and the dynamics in which text production occurs.

Research adopting an *Interpretive Structuralism* approach focuses on the analysis of the discourse supporting the social context. Studies that adopt this perspective are aimed at understanding the context and describing the broader picture of the organizational discursive context. Similar to socio-linguistic studies, the interpretative structuralism approach to discourse is mainly constructivist and aims to understand the ways in which an organization's broader discursive context is constructed, without considering the power struggles that may arise between multiple social perspectives.

Among the different studies that use an interpretative structuralism approach, O'Connor (2000) studied organizational change in a high-technology research setting, examining how narratives were used by managers to make the change necessary and real.

Perhaps *Critical Discourse Analysis (CDA)* represents the most widespread and influential theoretical approach used to analyse organizational discourse. According to CDA, any text is the product of a process of interdiscursivity and intertextuality, in which multiple understandings and discourses merge, collide and are influenced, and thus, result in new texts that are produced from the transformation of original texts. In particular, CDA considers discourse as a form of social practice and emphasises how discursive activity constructs the social space in which the actors perform, through the formation of concepts, objects, and subject positions (Jorgensen and Phillips, 2002, p. 61).

In this regard, CDA is relevant since it goes beyond the simple examination of discourse as verbal and written utterances, toward a connection between the texts (both written and oral) and the social context in which they are produced. As mentioned by Hardy (2001), CDA moves past the linguistic approach to discourse analysis, looking at the constructive effects of discourse by questioning who is involved in a certain discourse, as well as how, why and when it is produced.

Similar to social linguistic analysis, *Critical Linguistic Analysis* also focuses on the content and meaning of texts, statements and discursive utterances. However, it also looks at the power relations that surround the production and consumption of texts (Anderson-Gough, Grey, and Robson, 2000). Therefore, Critical Linguistic Analysis could be seen as fitting somewhere between CDA and social linguistic analysis, since it looks at power dynamics, but focuses more closely on the micro-dynamics that take part in writing texts down.

As mentioned by Jorgensen and Phillips (2002), Critical Linguistic Analysis focuses on the analysis of specific pieces of text in order to understand how the structures of domination in the local or proximate context are implicated in that text (Jorgensen and Phillips, 2002). O' Connor (1995) used literary analysis and the study of rhetoric, narrative, and metaphor to explore how organizational change programs are implemented.

According to Critical Linguistic Analysis, what one knows about the world is not objective. Reality is only accessible to us through oral and written discourse and it is the product of the ways in which people categorise the understanding of the world in a certain time frame and context (Jorgensen and Phillips, 2002).

Among the different approaches described, Critical Discourse Analysis is fundamental for the purposes of this study because it does not focus on the investigation of discourse as linguistic analysis per se, instead it studies the complexity of the social relations that frame the development of discourse (Wodak and Meyer, 2009).

4.3. Critical Discourse Analysis

Critical Discourse Analysis (CDA) defines discourse as a form of social practice which both constitutes the social world and is constituted by other social practices (Jorgensen and Phillips, 2002, p. 61). Developed by Fairclough in 1992, CDA is based on Foucault's archaeological and genealogical studies of discourse and particularly on the effect of power relations and discrepancies in knowledge production (Fairclough, 1992; Phillips and Hardy, 2002; Wodak and Meyer, 2009).

Following Foucault's studies, Fairclough (1992) focuses on the role of discursive activity in constituting, sustaining and constraining conflicting power relations (Fairclough; 1992). CDA researchers analyse the struggles between multiple subject positions, exploring how some of them are privileged and some others are marginalized through discourses (Phillips and Hardy, 2002; Wodak and Meyer, 2009).

Three of the most significant theoretical insights of CDA are based on Foucault's earlier "archaeological" studies in which he describes discourses as constituting objects of knowledge, resulting from intertextuality and interdiscursivity, as well as forms of social practices.

According to Foucault, objects of knowledge do not exist independently from discourse production (Foucault, 1972). Instead, they are constituted and transformed into discourse according to rules and discursive formation. In this regard, discourses are meant to contribute to the production, transformation, and reproduction of the concepts, objects and, possibly, to subject positions that emerge in social life (Fairclough, 1992).

The other common aspect of CDA and Foucauldian studies relates to the spatial and time frame interdependence between different discourse practices. According to Foucault, the production of texts is inevitably affected by prior texts (intertextuality) and at the same time it affects the interpretation of future texts (interdiscursivity).

Another aspect of Foucauldian studies that influence the CDA approach is related to the definition of discourse as being a form of social practice that reproduces and changes knowledge, identities and social relations, including power relations. In this way, discourses structure the social space for action. As new texts are produced, discourses evolve, leading to changes in the concepts, objects, subject positions and the power relations that characterize the social context.

Foucault (1979) conceives of power as embedded in discourse and any discourse constitutes a system of power. Moreover, Foucault considers knowledge production as a process that always takes place through power relations. According to Foucault, power has no "essence". It is not representable in pure form, but functions as a commodity that is employed and exercised within social relations (Foucault, 1977, p. 89). In Foucauldian terms, then, power comes out through discursive and social practices and, at the same time, constitutes and affects individual positions and may impede, as well as empower, those who take part in the discourse (Hardy and Phillips, 2004). In this regard, power is not negative, nor necessarily positive, but productive. It not only excludes, represses, censors, masks or conceals, but "power produces; it produces reality; it produces domains of objects and rituals of truth" (Foucault 1979, p. 194).

The Foucauldian conception of power and its embeddedness in discourse has been explored by CDA studies that aim to explore power/knowledge relations as expressions of an individual's perspectives or of an idea's formulation within a certain historical and institutional context (Fairclough, 1992). As mentioned by Wodak and Meyer (2009):

> "while a Foucauldian view largely dismisses agency by self-interested actors, Critical Discourse Analysis suggests there is space for the use of power, albeit within a particular discursive context. This space and the exercise of the power associated with positions within a discourse provide the potential for possible change in discourses over time" (p.11).

In particular, CDA describes discourses and the contexts in which they are determined, such as organizations, "not simply as social collectives, where shared meaning is produced, but rather as sites of struggle where different groups compete to shape the social reality of organizations in ways that serve their own interests" (Mumby and Clair, 1997, p. 182). For CDA, discursive differences are negotiated through the texts that are produced and the conversations that the actors have had.

> "Therefore, texts are often sites of struggle in that they show traces of differing discourses and ideologies contending and struggling for dominance" (Wodak and Meyer, 2009, p. 11).

In this regard, Phillips and Hardy (2004) developed a model that explores how discourses constitute power relationships and, furthermore, how power struggles are apparent in a social context in which texts are produced, transmitted and consumed.

4.3.1. The realm of discourse: concepts, objects and subject positions

Phillips and Hardy (2004) define the realm of discourse as a site where texts are produced, transmitted, and consumed through discourse and power relations. According to Phillips and Hardy (2004), discourses operate as sites in which power positions interact and where processes of interpretation are enacted by associating discursive concepts, objects and subject positions (see Figure 4.2).

Figure 4.2 – The relationship between concepts, objects and subject positions (Phillips and Hardy, 2004 p. 301).

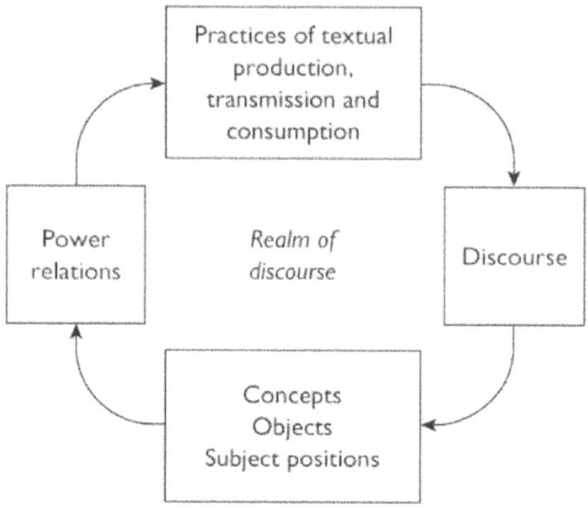

Concepts refer to the ideal understandings that come from text production and conversations in certain contexts (Fairclough, 1992; Hardy *et al.*, 2000). They are described as "categories, relationships and theories through which [one] understands the world and relates to one another" (Fairclough, 1992, p. 46). These concepts reside in the realm of "ideas" but have effects in the material world as they provide meanings to social actions. Due to their inherent nature as ideas, discursive concepts have no fixed meaning and are considered to be contextual and time related. This contextual and time-related nature stimulates debates and contestations among the people involved in their understanding, which unfolds through the ongoing construction of texts. Concepts are contested due to their ideal, cultural and historical character. They are dependent on discourse and influence individual understandings of the world, which may change over time and from social group to social group (Hardy and Phillips, 1999).

According to Phillips and Hardy (1997), concepts also have material implications. While some concepts exist only in the expressive order (for example, abstract concepts), others are attached to a material referent. Then, concepts that have a material existence are referred to as objects (Hardy and Phillips, 1999). In this study, for instance, sustainability as a concept gains meaning and materiality through sustainability accounting and reporting, which conversely contribute to making sense of what sustainability means within organisations. Thus, objects make sense in terms of the concepts that are applied to them. According to Chia (2000), discourse gives sense to the material world and makes it real by naming, labelling, classifying and thereby attaching concepts to undefined objects. Concepts affect the way in which objects are understood and socially embedded (Phillips and Hardy, 1997). The main difference between discursive concepts and objects resides in the tangibility and "shapes" of ideas. Concepts exist solely in the realm of ideas, while objects are part of the practical order and exist in the material world. Concepts do not have form until discursive objects mould them into practices by objectifying them (i.e. translating them into physical/visible objects). Objects are not pre-existing or fixed, rather, they are temporary patterns "constituted by and shaped from micro-interactions as actors perform their everyday work" (Thomas *et al.* 2011, p. 22). Also, objects are contextual and may change over time depending on the ideals, theories and understandings (concepts) that are attached to them. However, as suggested by Hardy and Thomas (2015), objects serve to inscribe bodies, produce identities, and implicate subjects in a recursive relationship between objects and individuals (Hardy and Thomas, 2015, p. 688).

Individual interactions and interpretations are thus fundamental to the constitution of objects and result from the "joint mediation between the built-in properties of objects and the intentions and purposes of human subjects" (Fairhurst and Putnam, 2004, p. 18). Individuals do not join discourse and social interactions as stable entities. When individuals take part in discourse, they position themselves and construct their own subjectivities. They are products of interaction and are continually recreated and challenged through discourse.

In this regard, Hardy (2004) maintains that "discourse helps to construct organizational reality by shaping the ways in which issues can be talked about, how individuals conduct themselves in relation to certain issues, and the knowledge that is constructed about them. By creating objects of knowledge, categories of social subjects, forms of self, social relationships, and conceptual frameworks, discourse acts as a powerful ordering force in organizations" (Hardy, 2004, p. 416). In this regard, through discourse, concepts, objects and subject positions are inextricably related to each other and can be very hard to distinguish (Oswick, 2000). Also, these interrelations depend on the ways in which multiple subject positions interact with each other to give meaning to an organization's aspects and initiatives.

From this perspective, subject positions, as well as objects, are produced through social interactions. Subject positions then are social products and at the same time emerge from the ongoing struggle that discourses produce (Phillips and Hardy, 1997, p. 168). Subject positions are shaped, and at the same time shape, the contextual relations, objects and concepts within which discourse takes place due to the power positions they hold

(Foucault, 1972 pp. 95-96). As mentioned by Maguire and Hardy (2013), anything that we think exists in reality, emerges from interactive and productive (also organizing) processes, through which particular meanings are attributed (Maguire and Hardy, 2013).

Further, Hall (1997) maintain that "meaning does not inhere in things, in the world. It is constructed, produced; it is the result of a signifying practice – a practice that produces meaning, that makes things mean" (p. 24). These studies acknowledge that meaning cannot be fixed, but it is socially constructed and unfolds in practice through discourse (oral or written text). Social context and social practice are, therefore, an integral part of discourses, which actively shape "the world around us by providing conceptual guidance for actions" (Spence, 2007, p. 858).

4.4. Summary and some further thoughts

Although it is impossible for the concept of sustainability to achieve closure and therefore be 'defined' (through, for example, accounting and reporting practices), the ongoing attempt to give it meaning produces different discourse, ways of talking about, understanding and interpreting its content. Such discourses have both reflective and constructive power, which suggests that, rather than searching for a bounded definition of sustainability, more attention should be given to the enabling process that its unbounded nature stimulates.

The following chapter describes in-depth the methodology adopted to address the objectives of this study using the theoretical framework outlined in this chapter.

Chapter 5
METHODOLOGY

SUMMARY: 5.1. Discourse analysis as a methodological approach. – 5.2. Data collection strategy. – 5.3. The case of DAPHNE. – 5.4. Data collection and analysis. – 5.5. Summary and further thoughts.

5.1. Discourse analysis as a methodological approach

Chapter Four referred to "discourses" or "discourse analysis" as a theoretical approach that covers an extremely wide variety of studies, ranging from conversation analysis, interactional social linguistics, critical discourse analysis and critical linguistics, to name a few. [1]

Phillips and Hardy (2002) suggest that the most important contribution of discourse analysis is that it examines how language constructs a phenomenon – not how it reflects and reveals it. Thus, discourse analysis provides a more profound interrogation of how socially produced ideas and objects are created, held in place, and populate organisational contexts over time (Grant *et al.*, 2004). As an interpretative research approach, discourse analysis endeavours to uncover the way in which a certain concept attains meaning and is produced in practice (Phillips and Hardy, 2002, p. 6).

The analysis of how discourse is used to construct a certain version of reality and why it is being used in this way can be carried out through text or several language utterances, depending on the scope and scale of the research (Dick, 2004; p. 207). Thus, different methods of data gathering and analysis can be used from study to study.

Furthermore, throughout the analysis of texts, researchers are required to examine what concepts are produced, what subject positions were involved, and how concepts were translated into objects (Phillips *et al.* 2008).

Fairclough (1992) provides some guidelines for exploring how discourse constructs reality, by examining the following points: 1) the actual content, structure and meaning of the text under analysis; 2) how discursive practices produce and consume texts through discursive interaction, as well as communicate meaning and beliefs; 3) the social context and practices through which these interactions take place (Fairclough, 1992, p. 72).

---

[1] See Chapter Four for further investigation.

According to Fairclough, each of these dimensions requires a different kind of analysis, such as text analysis (description), processing analysis (interpretation), social analysis (explanation) (see Figure 5.1).

Figure 5.1 – Three-dimensional conception of discourse (Fairclough, 1992 p. 73).

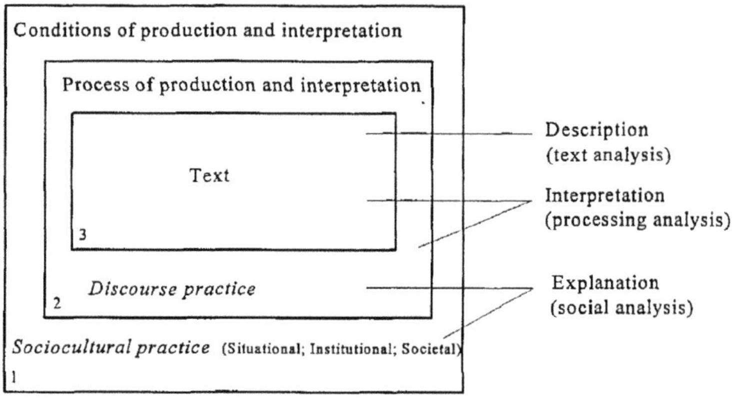

5.2. Data collection strategy

As highlighted in the previous chapters, undefined concepts such as sustainability can be filled with ever-unfolding meanings through the discourses that these meanings are a part of and also through the social practices that they shape and of which they are constituted (Laine, 2005). Therefore, the ongoing attempt to give meaning to concepts, such as sustainability, and represent it through accounting and reporting practices, may lead to multiple 'discourses' about sustainability, i.e. different ways of talking about, understanding and interpreting its content.

A significant gap still exists between what it means to be sustainable and how organisations attempt to represent and communicate it to external shareholders and stakeholders. As highlighted from some studies in the literature, the development of organisational texts such as sustainability reports and, more recently, Integrated Reports are of primary interest for case study research (de Villiers *et al.*, 2014; Eccles and Krzus, 2014; 2010; Simnett and Huggins, 2015; Dumay *et al.*, 2016) since they represent the primary internal and external communication systems in which discussions surrounding organisational financial and non-financial performance take place (Tregidga *et al.* 2014).

Considering the need to explore how sustainability accounting and reporting are produced within organizations and with the aim to achieve the research objective, this study investigates and intrinsically explain how sustainability becomes meaningful within organisations.

In particular, the case of DAPHNE,[2] has been chosen as a suitable site because of its "typical" explorative activities in the oil and gas industry, which make it necessary to assess and find a balance between financial and non-financial performance; environmental, social, political, geographical and financial risks; as well as the long-term effects of short-term decisions (i.e. evaluation of externalities). Further, DAPHNE was chosen from a variety of companies operating in the oil and gas sector because of its role as a company leader in the pilot program launched by the International Integrated Reporting Council (IIRC) in 2010. DAPHNE's participation in the pilot programme was considered a critical issue when choosing the case study because since 2010 the company's approach to sustainability reporting radically changed by combining sustainability and profitability issues into a single process and ultimately in a single report. As a result of its participation in this pilot program, DAPHNE commenced a process of integrated thinking and reporting that required a cultural shift by the units involved in the annual report preparations. The development of integrated thinking and reporting also influenced the strategic plan and the accounting practices used to contextually monitor sustainability and financial performance.

The following section introduces explains briefly DAPHNE's approach to sustainability and integrated reporting, which will be analysed in further detail in Chapters Six.

5.3. The case of DAPHNE

DAPHNE is one of the largest oil and gas companies operating in more than 70 countries around the world, with a workforce of approximately 35,000 people. Along the entire value chain, DAPHNE has significant responsibilities for minimising the impact of its extractive activities.

Similar to many oil and gas companies (see, e.g., IPIECA, 2015), sustainability has been a key aspect of DAPHNE's business model, strategic planning and reporting system since its establishment. DAPHNE's inclusive business purposes and strategic approach to sustainable value creation is operationalized across the whole value chain and is based on three strategic drivers: 1) improving local countries' competences and socio-economic wealth; 2) maintaining and developing in-house competencies; 3) preventing, managing and mitigating risks of different natures.

---

[2] DAPHNE is a pseudonym used for reasons of privacy and confidentiality.

Furthermore, sustainability reporting practices have been in use since the mid-1990s, when DAPHNE started publishing an environmental report aimed at providing more effective communication of information regarding the environmental impact of its business activities. From 2006, a sustainability report was prepared in accordance with the Global Reporting Initiative, (e.g. see DAPHNE environmental and sustainability report 2006; 2007; 2008; 2009; 2010).

In 2011, DAPHNE began its journey toward Integrated Reporting by participating in the Pilot Program launched by the International Integrated Reporting Council (IIRC). In this context, DAPHNE's Sustainability Unit was required to integrate the company's sustainability and annual financial report into one single document. In 2012, following the IIRC's (International Integrated Reporting Council) guiding principles, DAPHNE published its first Integrated Report, within which the traditional annual report structure was combined with specific sections regarding DAPHNE's social and environmental strategies, performance and impacts.

Given the nature of DAPHNE's business, the importance of sustainability issues and the longevity of its voluntary reporting process on sustainability, this organisation offers an interesting setting for the purposes of this study. As an oil and gas company, DAPHNE has been involved in the process of measuring, controlling and justifying its environmental, social and economic impacts on the countries in which it operates for more than 20 years. Consequently, DAPHNE has been required to continually change and modify its performance measurement and reporting practices regarding sustainability in order to determine the main performance for sustainability that will positively or negatively affect the capacity of the organization to create sustainable value in the long term.

The following sections indicate how data have been collected and subsequently analysed to achieve the research objectives.

5.4. Data collection and analysis

The research analysis was structured by focusing on the contents of published reports (e.g. DAPHNE's CSR, sustainability and Integrated Reports) to explore how the concept of sustainability was represented and how its meaning evolved over time according to the development of the reporting process.

The analytical phase focused on the role that corporate reporting practices, and particularly integrated reporting, play in the attempt to represent sustainability within organizations. To investigate how the concept of sustainability was represented and the mechanism that corporate reporting practices trigger as they attempt to represent sustainability within organizations, DAPHNE sustainability reporting process has been explored and the evolution of the meaning of sustainability since 1996 (around 20 years) when the first Health, Safety and Environmental (HSE) report was published.[3]

Although social and environmental issues were part of DAPHNE's business approach since mid 1950s, the development of the sustainability report (from 1996 to 2009) and the introduction of integrated reporting (from 2010 to 2015) had a relevant role in figuring out what was meant to be sustainable for the business. Consequently, it has been explored how the meaning of sustainability was represented through sustainability reports (or similar such as Health, Safety and Environmental; Corporate Social Responsibility; and most recently Integrated Reports) by shedding light on how these practices contributed to making sustainability issues and performance more identifiable and visible within DAPHNE.

DAPHNE's sustainability and integrated reports have been chronologically analysed (Yin, 2004, p. 126) through a time ordered matrix (Miles and Huberman, 1994 p. 119) and classified in three periods (e.g. from 1996 to 2005; from 2006 to 2009; from 2010 to 2015). In each period the following issues have been analysed: 1) how sustainability was represented through reports and the meanings that these representations entailed; 2) the main social context and external contingencies that influenced the evolution of sustainability reporting within DAPHNE; 3) the key practices used; and 4) the units responsible for the preparation of the reports. Evidence from the data analysed and the related matrix is reported in chapter six.

5.5. Summary and further thoughts

This chapter describes the research design, data collection and data analysis. The methodological approach explained in this chapter is relevant to the aims of the research, because it allows the micro (textual) and macro context (organisation's institutional context) to be linked and enables the investigation of knowledge production of abstract understandings such as sustainability. Considering the interpretive nature of the methodology used, this study investigates texts, concepts and social interactions (Fairclough,

[3] This research focuses on published reports because, when asking managers about how sustainability was defined and represented within the organization, they mainly referred to the company's sustainability and/or integrated reports.

1992) that characterize the way in which a multinational organisation, such as DAPHNE, plans, measures and reports its annual sustainability performance.

As argued by Fairclough and Wodak (1997), "discourse is not produced without context and cannot be understood without taking context into consideration" (p. 277).

The results of the research are discussed in the following chapter.

Chapter 6
FROM SUSTAINABILITY TO INTEGRATED REPORTING: A JOURNEY OF 20 YEARS

6.1. DAPHNE's approach to sustainability and the evolution of sustainability reporting

Since its establishment in the early 1950s, DAPHNE's sustainability approach was aimed at promoting key business alliances with international producer countries by investing in proprietary technologies and training initiatives for local employees. DAPHNE's commitment to the host countries' requests contributed to an increase in the number of agreements signed with international institutions, thereby improving the exploration and production of oil and gas worldwide (in South America, Africa, and the Middle-east). For instance, in 1962, DAPHNE built its first company health centre and a training centre for African personnel.

From the 1970s to the 1980s, DAPHNE was required to improve its investments in research and development, thereby launching new operating programs for the exploration of renewable resources and in the field of energy savings.

In the early 1990s, increased market globalisation required companies to find a balance between competitiveness, economic growth, increased consumption, improved standards of living of the social community, as well as respect for the territory and environmental quality. Also, in 1992 the U.N. Earth Summit in Rio de Janeiro increased companies' awareness about the necessity to measure and communicate how traditional business activities affect the environment and the society as a whole. In particular, it was recognized that the oil industry plays a leading role in sustainable development and economic growth by promoting innovative technological solutions for exploring and extracting energy resources that have a lower environmental impact. This period coincided with an increasing international expansion and liberalization of trade and capital markets, privatizations and deregulation of economic activities, with a rapid expansion of new information through communication technologies.

To react to the increase in external competition, DAPHNE began a profound transformation in the governance and organizational structure of the company from 1996 to 2001. DAPHNE's internal management and external compliance evolved rapidly, due to increasing interactions with public bodies, institutions, and the media that was more interested in the company's performance and achievements towards global sustainable development.

DAPHNE's approach to environmental, social and economic issues steadily evolved throughout this period, including the accounting and reporting practices that were implemented.

To describe how the meaning of sustainability evolved within DAPHNE, including the evolution of the accounting and reporting practices adopted, in this chapter three main evolutionary phases have been identified. The three phases have been analysed according to the effect of contextual initiatives and regulations; the nature of the report produced; the key practices used in order to represent sustainability performance within the report; as well as the unit responsible for the production of the report.

The first phase started in 1996 and concluded in 2005 when the company's reporting approach was reviewed due to the external pressures dictated by its international expansion and privatization process. In this first phase, DAPHNE developed the first version of the health, safety and environmental report, providing some information on the company's impacts on the environment and the health and safety of the employees. The second evolutionary phase of sustainability reporting began in 2006 and concluded in 2009, during which the institutionalisation of globally accepted sustainability guidelines and standards from international initiatives and regulatory institutions (e.g. GRI, UN Global Compact) resulted in the publishing of DAPHNE's first "sustainability" report. In this second phase, the meaning of sustainability became more formalized within the organization's reporting process, combining health, safety and environmental issues with the corporate approach on social responsibility. The third and last evolutionary phase began in 2010 and concluded in 2015. This reporting phase coincided with the implementation of integrated reporting, in order to better measure and communicate how key sustainability initiatives, objectives and performance affect the organization's strategic approach and long-term value creation.

6.2. Phase One – from 1996 to 2005: sustainability as an environmental and social concept

The transformations that DAPHNE underwent between the mid-1990s and the early 2000s, along with the changes that had taken place in the global economic system, have led the company towards broader levels of autonomy and different institutional responsibilities because of its new structure as a private company, and its exposure to international competition and interaction with society, such as public opinion, public bodies, institutions, the media and communities. The institutional context in which DAPHNE was operating at that time was characterised by increasing attention to the effects of corporate activities on the environment and to the necessity to manage and report them. In particular, as an oil and gas company, DAPHNE was required to extend its communication practices to better account and report the environmental, health and safety performances achieved during each year.

In 1996, DAPHNE published its first report on health, safety and the environment (HSE) and was one of the first companies in Europe to create its own norms of self-regulation by issuing a set of principles and guidelines (i.e. "Code of practice"), to encourage an ethical, decision-making approach.[1] DAPHNE's report was produced on a yearly basis, illustrating primarily how company initiatives affected environmental development, with a focus on the activities of the upstream segment of the value chain.

Between 1996 and 2002, DAPHNE's approach to sustainability was meant to combine the issues and the performances that were related to the impacts of the organization's operations on the environment and on the safeguard of the health and safety of the employees. The emergence of an increased number of international institutions that regulate corporate voluntary reporting,[2] together with the exceptional participation of a wide number of companies in the U.N. Johannesburg Summit in 2002, contrib-

---

[1] The Code of Practice was developed to direct DAPHNE's management decisions in a series of key areas such as business ethics, transparency and correctness in accounting and reporting, industrial relations, health, safety and environmental protection, with the aim of improving employees' professional development, stimulate dialogue and mutual respect with local partners in order to develop DAPHNÈs socio-environmental sustainability of the company's operations in the host-countries' territories.

[2] For further information on the topic, please take a look at Chapter 2.

uted to improving the scope of DAPHNE's HSE reporting process. Consequently, more emphasis was given to the impact of the organizational activities on the social community and internal workplace.[3 4]

At the group level, an HSE department was created to define and update the Group Code of Practice guidelines; ensure the coordination of HSE management systems; audit the effectiveness of HSE management in the business areas and consolidate HSE performance indicators; define sustainability strategy and develop coherent initiatives; as well as promote the dissemination of information and best practices (DAPHNE, 2001).

A data base was developed to better control the data input of the reporting process, building up a statistical series for both consolidated and individual companies, as well as developing trend analysis. In 2001, HSE data were collected and reported by approximately 260 units, operating in more than 65 countries around the world.

The establishment of the HSE department also incentivized the development of an experimental HSE reporting system that was organized around four management processes: planning, implementation, control and corrective actions, and management review (see Figure 6.1).[5]

Furthermore, the HSE management system was implemented internally by DAPHNE's business segments to take account of the specific needs of the operative context; keep DAPHNE's corporate management up to date on HSE performance; and ensure the achievement of pre-established targets.

---

[3] In 2001 DAPHNE signed a protocol of intentions with partner companies to improve the control of environmental performance and health care in the workplace (DAPHNE, 2001). This protocol was aimed at stimulating managers' consultation and collection of information on the following issues: training, health, safety and environment, international industrial relations and employee shareholding.

[4] DAPHNE, (2001), Health and Safety Report.

[5] The planning process was aimed at defining the objectives and schedules, technical, professional and financial resources to be included in the following four-year strategic plan. The implementation process comprised three further sub-categories: 1) the development of pre-arranged activities to ensure the achievement of HSE improvement objectives that were included in the strategic plan and the operative control of the HSE performance of business activities; 2) the emergency preparedness, which was dependent on the level of contingency planning; reporting and communication activities; 3) the involvement of employees, external parties and other stakeholders (such as local communities, governments, institutions and associations) in the pursuit of HSE objectives, also with regard to the company's commitment and results. The control process required the monitoring of annual HSE targets and objectives for identifying eventual corrective actions through continuous auditing and reporting. The management review process completed the HSE management system cycle and was developed in two activities: an analysis of the gap between results and targets; and the definition of objectives for the subsequent cycle (DAPHNE, 2001).

Figure 6.1 – DAPHNE's prototypal HSE management system (Source adapted from DAPHNE's HSE report, 2002 p. 15)

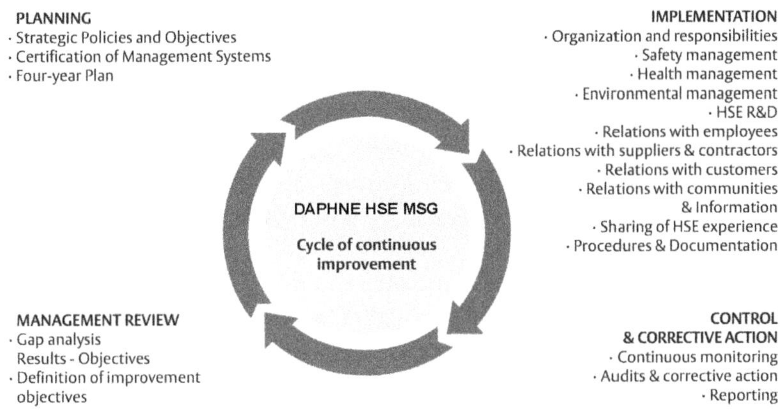

In 2002, DAPHNE created a Corporate Social Responsibility (CSR) unit to support the already existing HSE department in managing sustainability issues, performance, and impacts of the initiatives that cut across different areas of the business. The CSR unit promoted cohesiveness and awareness among the different organizational areas and dialogue with external stakeholders on the following issues: Human Resources, Security, Health Safety and Environment, Customer and Supplier Relations.

With the establishment of the new CSR unit, the HSE report was substituted by a Corporate Responsibility report in 2003 (also for 2004 and 2005), which focused mainly on DAPHNE's respect for individuals, health and safety in the workplace, dialogue with labour representatives and on the development of the territories that host DAPHNE's operations.

The development of the CSR reporting process within DAPHNE was favoured by the occurrence of a growing number of international initiatives and regulations that required companies in the oil and gas industry to provide transparent communications about their responsibilities regarding social and environmental impacts, as well as explain how they operate to fulfil social demands (e.g. IPIECA and The Global Reporting Initiative sector supplement). In particular, multinational companies were expected to contribute to the development and economic growth of the poorest countries by offering new models of cooperation and promoting growth, progress and achievement of local people potentials (DAPHNE, 2003).

In 2003, the concept of sustainability gained a new meaning by focusing on "the adoption of socially responsible business conduct"[6] and by giving higher

[6] Corporate Responsibility report 2003, p. 9.

emphasis to the social development of the communities in the developing countries in which DAPHNE was operating at that time (DAPHNE, 2003).[7]

The new approach to sustainability as a corporate social responsibility issue also influenced the contents published in the report, giving higher relevance to the company's respect for the development of individuals by focusing on the company's workforce safety and health, and the respect and development of the territory. However, environmental, social, health and safety initiatives, although being recognised as part of the company's code of practice and corporate social responsibility, were still represented separately in the report.

The following chart briefly illustrates the evolving meaning of sustainability within DAPHNE from 1996 to 2005, according to the contextual initiatives that took place in that period; the nature of the report produced; the key practices used and the units responsible for the preparation of the report (See Figure 6.2).

As explained in the following section, some of the most significant developments in terms of sustainability reporting within DAPHNE took place in the period between 2006 and 2015 when the meaning of sustainability gained greater importance within the company's initiatives and business model.

Figure 6.2 – The evolution of the meaning of sustainability from 1996 to 2005

The evolution of sustainability reporting in DAPHNE	**From 1996 to 2005**		
External contingencies	• Globalization and internationalization of Oil and Gas companies • Privatization process of the company from 1996 to 2001	• Rio + 10, UN Earth Summit in Johannesburg, 2002 • Introduction of international regulations and guidelines on Corporate Social Responsibility (i.e. GRI and Global Compact)	
Meanings of Sustainability	**1996-2002:** Sustainability as combining environmental and Health and Safety issues disconnected from traditional business objectives		**2003-2005:** Sustainability as Corporate Social Responsibility, introducing the importance of stakeholders' engagement
Report	Health and safety and Environmental report		Corporate Social Responsibility Report
Key practices used	HSE Management System		
Unit responsible for the preparation of the report		• HSE Department in 2001	• CSR unit in 2003

[7] Terms such as "Sustainability", "Sustainable development" and "Sustainable value" appeared 79 times in 81 pages of the report.

6.3. Phase two – from 2006 to 2009: connecting environmental, social and economic performance in a sustainability report

The increasing pressures from external stakeholders and political institutions who were asking for more transparent reporting processes highlighted the inconsistencies between existing corporate social responsibility reporting practices, the broader evolution of the organizational activity and the external socio-contextual environment. Considering the increasing necessity to understand the role of organizations in the achievement of sustainable development, national institutions and regulators have developed guidelines, principles and standards to enhance organizations' accounting and reporting in this regard (e.g. Global Compact, Global Reporting Initiative guidelines).

During this second evolutionary phase of reporting, "sustainability" within DAPHNE gained further meaning by combining economic, social and environmental issues within the same reporting system and considering sustainable development as a target to be pursued by involving internal and external stakeholders within the company's decision-making process. [8]

To strengthen the company's positioning and reputation towards sustainable development, in 2006 DAPHNE consolidated its relations and memberships with some leading rating agencies on sustainability performance and reporting, such as the Dow Jones Sustainability index.

The development of the first sustainability report in 2006 contributed to reinforce the company's commitment to sustainable development, promoting DAPHNE's stakeholder engagement and the involvement of the Board of Directors towards the achievement of long-term sustainability objectives. Higher relevance was given to the role of stakeholders for the company, formally taking into consideration not only their expectations but also actively involving them in the implementation and development of DAPHNE's sustainability principles and initiatives. In particular, a list of stakeholders who were interested in the company's activity towards sustainable development was illustrated, explaining for each the dialogue initiatives adopted (DAPHNE, 2006; p. 24). Also, the structure of the report changed, highlighting the challenges of sustainability that most affect DAPHNE's operations, from the upstream to the downstream; the company's governance structure and management system approach to sustainability; the company's commitments towards sustainable development and future expectations and strategies.

[8] DAPHNE, 2006; Sustainability report; p. 5.

In order to make sustainability issues and objectives relevant for all organizational subunits, in February 2006, DAPHNE launched a project called "Leadership and sustainability". The project was aimed at stimulating participants' reflection on the ethical component of usual managerial decisions, outlining a shared vision of sustainability and providing further information on the existing connection between sustainability initiatives, decision-making processes and managerial action.

From the development of the project on "Leadership and Sustainability", two main outputs were produced. First, in June 2006, the CSR unit and the HSE department were integrated into a new "Sustainability Unit" that was responsible for the preparation of internal and external reports on sustainability, in coordination with other guidelines and reporting tools provided by the CFO. A foundation was also created to promote and manage the development of projects and philanthropic initiatives in favour of host countries' wellbeing and life quality, and to prevent poverty and social exclusion.

Second, sustainability objectives were included in the annual master plan. DAPHNE's commitments and action for sustainable development were set forth and approved by the Board of Directors as part of the Strategic Plan for 2007-2010, and in March 2007 the principles were approved for the organizational model for sustainability, which became fully operative by 2008.

A first illustration of the company's strategic approach to sustainability was represented in 2007, highlighting the main drivers (e.g. People, Environment, Territory and Communities, Customers, Technological Innovation, Climate Change and Energy Efficiency that affect DAPHNE's business model to innovate over time and to invest in new technologies (see Figure 6.3). These were all surrounded by adequate governance guidelines and stable relations with external stakeholders.

Building on the managerial experience gained through the prototypal implementation of the HSE management system in 2002, DAPHNE presented its reviewed, sustainable reporting process and introduced the HSE integrated management system in 2007 in order to support the reporting process and monitor sustainability initiatives and performance in accordance with the company's main business strategies. [9]

---

[9] The HSE integrated management system involved two levels of action: the first focused on the steering, coordination and monitoring of sector and corporate HSE departments; and the other on the technical-operational management of individual sites, which receive management guidelines and adapt them to fit their specific technical/plant/environmental situations (DAPHNE, 2007; pp. 22-23).

Figure 6.3 – DAPHNE's conceptual model of sustainability (Source adapted from DAPHNE's sustainability report, 2007 p. 15)

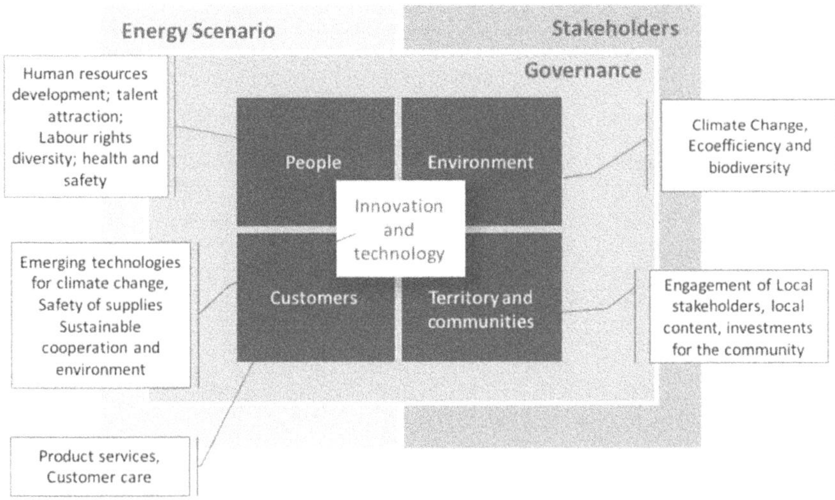

The sustainability report Implementation process was structured into three main processes: Planning, Control and Reporting (see Figure 6.4).

During the planning process, objectives and areas for sustainability that were relevant to the company's strategic plan were identified by the Sustainability Unit in conjunction with corporate departments and appropriate business areas.

In particular, managers of the corporate departments and business areas were responsible for managing, measuring and controlling sustainability project performance and targets on the basis of the guidelines issued by DAPHNE's CEO. Following the approval of the CEO, the corporate departments and business areas, together with the Sustainability Unit, were responsible for establishing the sustainability projects that were to be included in the ordinary planning and reporting processes.

During this process, managers were required to determine how their responsibilities for sustainability and business projects affected their appraisal and performance evaluation. As an incentive for achieving sustainability targets and objectives, top managers were evaluated according to the performance achieved that was in line with the group Sustainability results for the year and the Management by Objectives (MBOs) system.

The control process for sustainability projects was pursued by collecting and submitting the main sustainability KPIs of the projects to the attention of the Board of Directors and the CEO, who had a central role in determining the information to report in the Sustainability and Annual Report (reporting process).

Figure 6.4 – DAPHNE's sustainability process (Source adapted from DAPHNE's sustainability report 2007 p. 16)

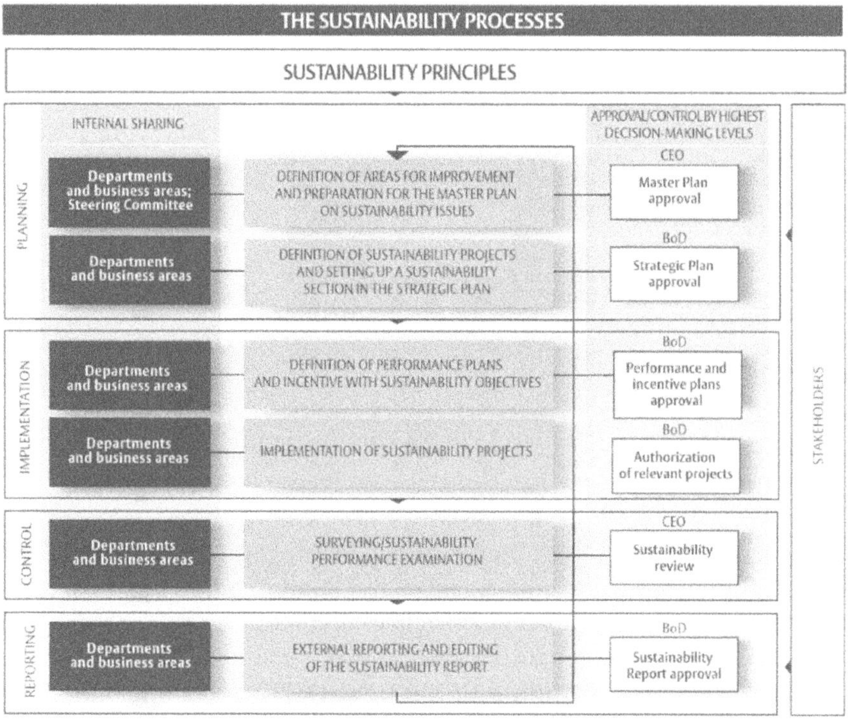

In 2008, DAPHNE's Sustainability process and HSE integrated management model became fully operational, involving different departments in the determination of the main organizations' sustainability objectives and targets. The completion of the full year management and reporting process contributed to identifying those initiatives that particularly influenced the organization's approach to sustainable value creation. Priority intervention areas, objectives and action plans for the four-year period from 2008 to 2012 were reviewed and implemented according to the suggestions of DAPHNE's main stakeholders.

Areas of improvement on the organization's sustainability initiatives were defined according to the main stakeholders' requests and the following four years of DAPHNE's strategic initiatives and objectives (2009-2012).

In contrast to the previous reporting versions, DAPHNE's 2008 sustainability report was completely restructured, giving higher importance to three macro areas: the contextual issues and future trends of the oil and gas industry, the corporate approach to sustainability issues and the relations with external stakeholders (e.g. customers, governments and local institutions).

Also, the 2008 sustainability model slightly changed its structure, by showing people training processes and internal development as central dimensions of the organization's sustainability model, together with innovation in research and development (see Figure 6.5).

Figure 6.5 – DAPHNE's sustainability model (Source adapted from DAPHNE's sustainability report 2008 p. 28)

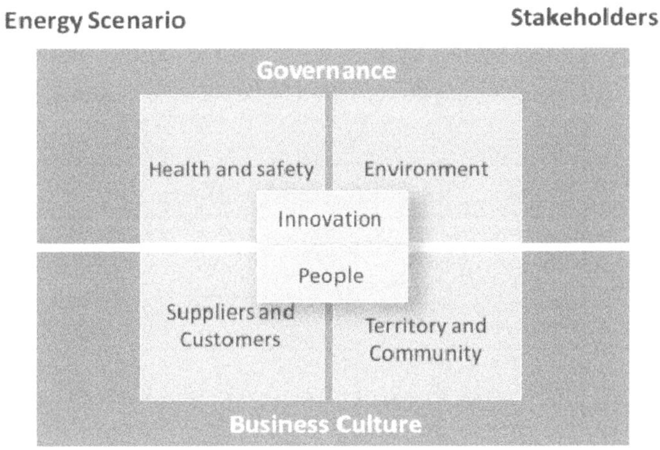

In 2009 the company decided to publish its last "sustainability" report (the last of its category) to leave space for a new form of report that would be able to illustrate the cause-effect relationships between financial and non-financial information. Because of the transitional role of the 2009 report, not many changes have been registered since 2008. The 2009 report mainly focused on the company's stakeholder engagement process, illustrating the key issues highlighted by the most relevant stakeholders and classifying them according to the company's main strategic objectives and materiality for the business. A materiality assessment was presented, analysing the relevance of each topic considered to be material according to the company's strategic objectives and the main stakeholders' expectations. The level of internal significance of the topics was determined by analysing the company's short, medium and long-term strategies, in light of the sustainability performance that was achieved in the past.

The chart below briefly illustrates the evolving process of sustainability within DAPHNE's reporting period from 2006 to 2009, according to the contextual initiatives that took place during that period; the nature of the report produced; the key practices used and the units responsible for the preparation of the report (see Figure 6.6).

Figure 6.6 – The evolution of the meaning of sustainability from 2006 to 2009

The evolution of sustainability reporting in DAPHNE	From 2006 to 2009		
External contingencies	• Incresased laws and regulations, both domestically and internationally (i.e. multiplicity of guidelines and directives on transparency of accounting practices for sustainability in Europe) • International stakeholders pressure for higher transparency. • Consolidated relations and memberships with some leading rating agencies on sustainability performance and reporting, such as the Dow Jones Sustainability index.		
Meanings of Sustainability	**2006-2009:** Sustainability does not make distinctions between Environmental and social issues. Sustainability gives name to the report.		
Report	Sustainability Report		
Key practices used	**2006** • Launch of the project on leadership and sustainability to stimulate participants reflections on ethical issues.	**2007** • First Sustainable Business Model published. • First Integrated Management Sustainability process developed.	**2008-2009** • The Integrated Management Sustainability process is fully operational. • Adoption of the GRI Materiality Matrix.
Unit responsible for the preparation of the report	The Sustainability Unit replaced the CSR unit and the HSE department		

In 2010, after having issued a series of sustainability reports, DAPHNE realized that the simple act of reporting data about the company sustainability initiatives was not enough. What was missing was a broader process of analysis and communication that would be able to illustrate the strategic leverages of the company towards sustainable value creation.

The following section describes DAPHNE's integrated reporting journey from 2010 to 2015, explaining how the meaning of sustainability has changed over time, also due to the application of this new reporting process.

6.4. Phase Three – from 2010 to 2015: integrating and connecting sustainability performance within DAPHNE's strategies

6.4.1. Applying integrated reporting within DAPHNE: combining sustainability and financial performance in the same report

In the aftermath of the financial crisis in 2008, the notion and functioning of capitalism, the ultimate purpose of the business, as well as the concept of corporate value creation have been questioned, together with the existing DAPHNE, principles, and practices used to manage and approach sustainable development.

External factors such as the evolution of national and international laws and regulations, (i.e. multiplicity of guidelines and directives on the transparency of accounting practices for sustainability in Europe, SEC guidelines and Dodd-Frank Act in the United States, Grenelle II act in France to name a few) required DAPHNE to improve its accounting and reporting system in order to clarify the connection between traditional business and sustainability performance in their annual reports. Additionally, the devastating accident of the British Petroleum deep-water platform in the Gulf of Mexico in late 2000, required oil and gas companies to demonstrate how the impacts generated by non-optimal management of intangibles on business results can affect the medium and long-term company reputation and financial viability.

It was around this time, that senior managers from different units in DAPHNE questioned the effectiveness of their existing sustainability reporting practices, with the intention of trying to better comprehend how and whether these practices were aligned with the main organization's strategies and objectives. Particularly, managers within DAPHNE's Sustainability Unit realized that a new approach was needed in order to communicate the ways in which sustainability and financial performance influence each other and the long-term viability of the business.

In 2010, the managers of the Sustainability Unit, in accordance with the Board of directors, discontinued the preparation of the sustainability report and adopted a prototype version of integrated report as their official Annual Report.

However, the absence of adequate principles, guidelines and reporting practices made the collection and representation of multiple performance factors in one report difficult. Indeed, the 2010 integrated annual report represented merely an embryonic attempt to put into one report a collage of information about the company's traditional and sustainability activities. The integrated reporting process became more structured in the following five years, in which new management accounting systems and key practices were adopted to improve the connectivity between financial and sustainability performance. This process required a reorganization of the business activities and a profound redefinition of DAPHNE's governance structure, decision-making processes, operating mechanisms, planning and monitoring systems.

With the implementation of the integrated reporting system, new rules and routines emerged to regulate the processes of gathering, collecting, accounting and reporting sustainability-related information. In particular, the involvement of different managers in the preparation of the integrated report, concurrently with the evolution of the IIRC international integrated reporting framework, contributed to the rethinking of DAPHNE's internal and external management and communicating process, thereby increasing the awareness of the link between financial and non-financial performance.

Also, DAPHNE's organizational structure changed, moving from a division-based structure to become streamlined and refocused on the priority of the company's core business. In 2013, a "sustainability and external scenarios committee" was established as part of the Board of Directors to instil and inspire the organizational culture of the importance of integrating financial and non-financial performance, as well as business and sustainability strategies, as two relevant issues in the company's decision-making process.[10]

Further reinforcement of DAPHNE's adoption of integrated reporting came from their participation in the 2011 pilot programme launched by the IIRC, which contributed to rethink and discuss the best practices for connecting financial and sustainability performance. Furthermore, a workgroup was created in 2011, gathering managers from different functions such as corporate planning, sustainability, external relations, corporate governance, and integrated risk management.

All these initiatives contributed to sharing and developing a new meaning for sustainability as being integrated within the business strategies and value creation. This new understanding of sustainability, as an integral part of the business objectives and strategies, also emerged from the accounting and reporting practices that the company used.

The 2011 version of the integrated report was a great improvement from that of 2010, giving details on DAPHNE's external scenario and industrial growth. Greater emphasis was given to the communication of the company's strategies for the following four years, the business model, governance and integrated risk management.

---

[10] A clear example of taking decisions according to the integration between business and sustainability strategies refers to the maximization of the company's industrial value and know-how. In the period between 2013-2015, DAPHNE restructured its assets in order to move to a low carbon approach of the business, transforming and enhancing most of its sites, which for 60 years had been part of the history of the company (see Section 6.5.3). In particular, DAPHNÈs strategy in Italy ranged from the consolidation of the Upstream sector, converting low-margin sites into bio-refineries, to refocus the exploration and production on specialties and green chemical products. The decisions made regarding this conversion combined the company's objective of profitability with the protection of employment levels and environmental preservation.

Differing from the sustainability business models seen in 2007 and 2008, DAPHNE's 2011 business model illustrated the strategic, organizational and sustainable aspects of the business and was designed around three circles framed by the organization's rules of corporate governance. The circles refer to the distinctive assets (i.e. value chain activities), strategic guidelines (i.e. drivers that lead to the creation of sustainable value), and pillars that influence the organization's ability to create value over the long term (see Figure 6.7).

Figure 6.7 – DAPHNE's integrated business model (Source adapted from DAPHNE's integrated report 2011)

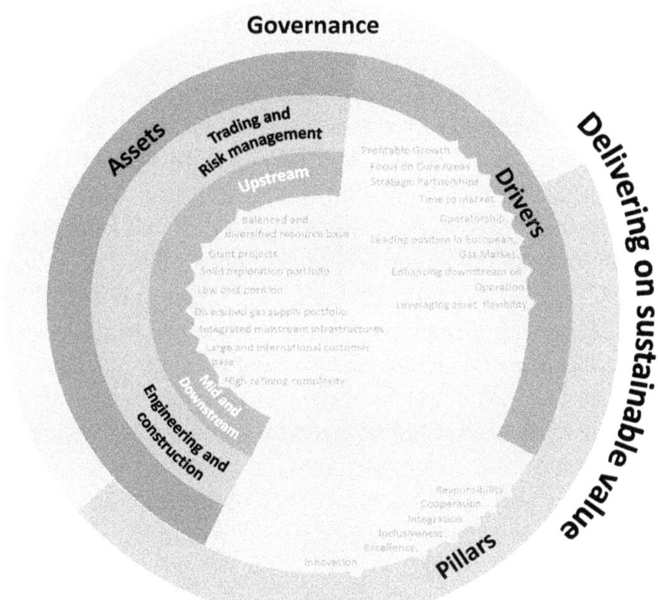

DAPHNE's integrated risk management model (IRM) represents the second most relevant practice presented in 2011, and broadly developed in 2012. The integrated risk management model was aimed at ordering, classifying and assessing the most relevant financial and non-financial risks that affect the company's sustainable value creation process. Based on the guidelines provided by the Board of Directors, the IRM model identifies, analyses and assesses the impact and probability of occurrence of risks according to the relevance to the country in which DAPHNE operates, regulatory developments, environment, finance, strategy and operations. The score attributed to each risk is then illustrated in a matrix that combines the probability of occurrence and its levels of impact through quantitative and qualitative parameters, which are continually monitored to identify areas of improvement; analyse risk evolution in terms of treatment measures and prevent the occurrence of potential new risks. The 2011 integrated report also introduced a specific section, entitled "Consolidated Sustainability Statement", in which the key performance indicators of social and environmental initiatives were illustrated.

In 2012, DAPHNE had to readapt its value chain activities to better address the three major shocks that affected the energy sector at that time, such as the collapse of gas consumption; the decline of oil demand and refining margins; and the dramatic fall of oil prices in Europe (DAPHNE, 2012). Also, the company's business model has been reviewed, considering the company's ability to deliver sustainable value as a central issue to be pursued.

The 2012 business model illustrates the company's governance structure and the integrated risk management process as the base for the main assets, drivers and strategies that characterize the company's ability to deliver sustainable value (see Figure 6.8). Within this description, sustainability issues are conceived as main drivers for achieving DAPHNE's business goals with a focus on exploration activity and replacement of reserves.

Although the implementation of integrated reporting in 2011 and 2012 contributed to spreading awareness about the necessity to understand the initiatives and drivers through which the company creates sustainable value in the long term, sustainability and financial performance were still represented as being separate from each other and not very connected. Financial and sustainability information was brought together in the same annual report but illustrated separately and matched as a collage of information and figures.

The absence of a framework or guidelines to support the preparation of the integrated report made the integration of different kinds of information difficult. Further, the increasing amount of information to collect and analyse made the internal communication process difficult between different functions and perspectives. These difficulties affected the length of the two reports published in 2011 and 2012, which were still quite long (around 260 pages). After the publication of the Integrated Reporting Framework in 2013, more efforts have been made in the development of a management control system able to represent the cause and effect relationship between financial and sustainability performance. In particular, to improve the connectivity between sustainability and financial performance towards the assessment of the sustainable value created by the company, between 2013 and 2015 the Sustainability Unit led the development of a prototypical project for integrated thinking and reporting, which was adopted at the group level in 2015.

Figure 6.8 – DAPHNE's integrated business model, 2012 (Source adapted from DAPHNE's integrated report 2012 p. 12)

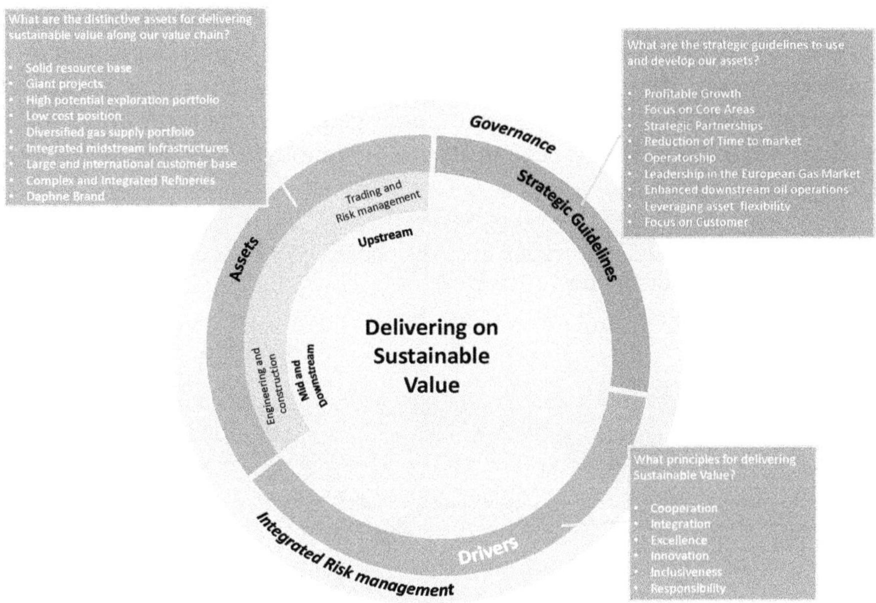

6.4.2. Connecting multiple perspectives and performance: the 2013-2015 integrated reporting development

The 2013 annual report was the third official integrated report published by DAPHNE and the first prepared in accordance with the guidelines and principles of the prototype framework published by the IIRC in December 2013. This integrated report described the competitive context, the main challenges of the market for each segment of the value chain (from the upstream to the downstream), the financial and non-financial performance achieved, and the related targets for the following three years (2014-2017).

Also, DAPHNE's business model was redesigned with the aim to illustrate how multiple sources of capital (i.e. capitals) affect the organization's strategies and sustainable value creation in the long term. [11] The

[11] Some of the most relevant KPIs per capital are illustrated along with the description of DAPHNE's value chain from the upstream to the mid-downstream. Concerning financial capital, the report provides some data about the net profit for the year compared to 2012, the net cash of operating activities and the dividends paid. Concerning manufacturing capital, data on the capital expenditures for 2013 and the hydrocarbon reserves discovered were provided. Also, the report gives some infor-

capitals (i.e. financial, manufacturing, intellectual, human, social and relationship, and natural) are represented as cutting across the business model and providing the basis for the achievement of the company's strategic guidelines, assets and drivers. For each capital, the report illustrates in a table the most relevant objectives, initiatives and actions that affect the company value creation process and, more generally, the value created for and perceived by multiple organizational stakeholders (see Figure 6.9 and 6.10).

Figure 6.9 – DAPHNE's integrated business model, 2013 (Source adapted from DAPHNE's integrated report 2013, p. 4)

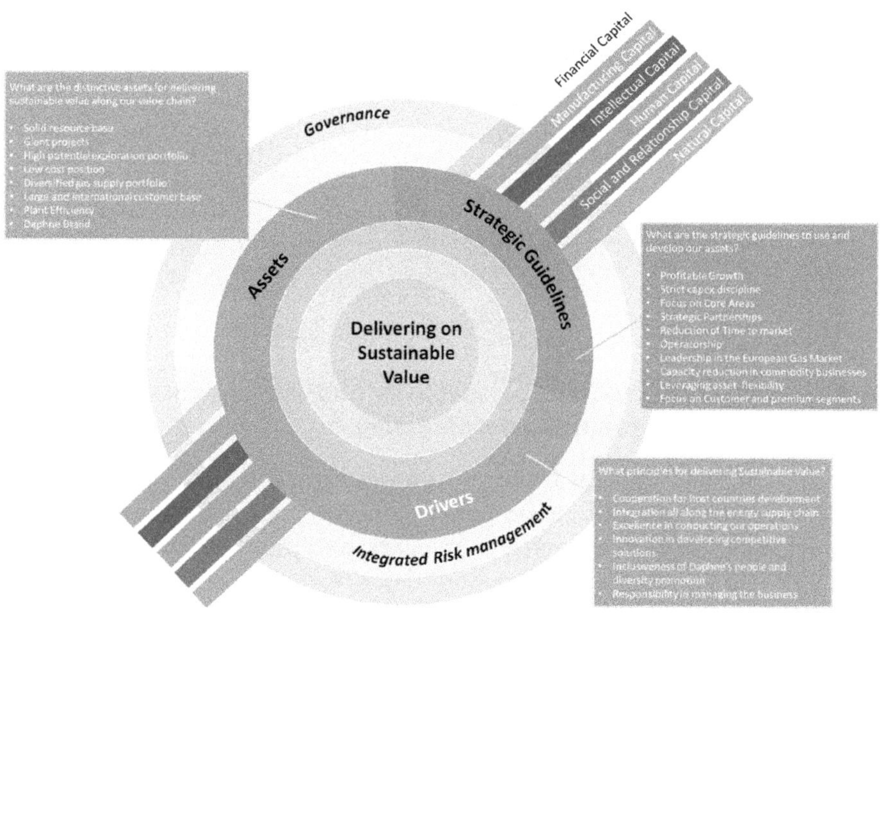

mation concerning the investments made in R&D and the number of patents detained. Concerning human capital, some data are provided regarding the percentage of employees hired during the year and the percentage of woman. Then concerning social and relationship capital, the report gives some data on the value of investments made in host countries. Some further data on the reduced number of oil spills and green-house gas (GHG) emissions, compared to the previous year, are provided to explain their impact on the environmental capital.

Figure 6.10 – DAPHNE's capitals, KPIs and strategic initiatives, 2013 (Source adapted from DAPHNE's integrated report, 2013 p. 5)

Daphne Initiatives/ Capitals	Stock of Capital	Daphne 's main Actions	Value Creation for Daphne	Value Creation for Daphne's Stakeholders
Financial Capital	• Financial Structure • Liquidity Reserves	• Cash Flow from Operations • Bank Loans • Bonds • Maintaining strategic Liquidity • Hedging • Dividends • Buyback • Working Capital Optimization	• Going Concern • Lower Cost of Capital • Reduction of Working Capital • Leverage Optimization • M&A Opportunities • Mitigation of Market Viability • Credit Worthiness	• Yields • Share Price appreciation • Social and Economic Growth • Satellite Activities
Productive Capital	• Onshore and Offshore Plants • Pipeline and storage plants • Liquefaction Plants • Refineries • Distribution Networks • Power Plants • Chemical Plants • Buildings and other equipment	• Technological Upgrade • Process Upgrade • Investments in new Businesses • Maintenance and development activities • Increase Environment Certifications	• Returns • Enlarging assets portfolio • Increase assets value • Reduction of Operational risks • Energy and operational efficiency • Reputation	• Availability of energy sources • Employment • Satellite Activities • Reduction of direct GHG emissions and responsible use of resources
Intellectual Capital	• Technologies and intellectual properties • Corporate internal procedures • Corporate governance Systems • Integrated Risk management • Management and control systems • Knowledge Management • ICT	• Research and development expenditures • Partnerships with center of excellence • Development of proprietary technologies • Application of procedures and systems • Audit	• Competitive Advantage • Risk mitigation • Transparency • Performance • Licence to Operate • Stakeholders' acceptability	• Reduction of Environmental and social impacts • Transfer of technologies and know-how to host countries • Contributing to the fight against corruption • Green Products
Human Capital	• People's Health and safety • Know-how and skills • Experience • Engagement • Diversity (Gender, seniority Geographical) • Daphne's thinking	• Safety at work • Recruiting, education and on the job training • Promotion of human rights • Daphne's people engagement • Knowledge management • Welfare • Leveraging on diversity • Enhancing individual talents and remuneration in accordance to a merit system	• Performance • Efficiency • Competitiveness • Innovation • Risk mitigation • Reputation • Talent Attraction	• Create employment and preserve jobs • Wellness of Daphne's people and communities • Increase and transfer know-how
Social and Relationship Capital	• Relationships with stakeholders (institutions, governments, communities, associations, customers, suppliers, NGOs, industrial partners, universities) • Daphne's brand	• Stakeholders' engagement • MoU with governments and Local authorities • Projects for local development and local content • Strategic partnerships • Involvement in international panel discussions • Development of programmes on research and training • Partnerships with trade unions • Quality of services rendered • Brand management	• Operational and social licence • Reduction of time to market • Country risk reduction • Market share • Alignment to international best practices • Reputation • Competitive advantage • Supplier reliability • Customer retention	• Local Socio- economic development • Customers and suppliers satisfaction • Share of expertise with territories and communities • Satisfaction and incentives for community • Promoting respects of Workers' rights
Natural Capital	• Oil&Gas reserves • Water • Biodiversity and ecosystems • Air • Soil	• Exploration, production, transporting, refining and distributing hydrocarbons • Investments in new businesses (Bio-refineries) • Investments in technological and process upgrades • Remediation activities	• Hydrocarbon reserve growth • Opex Reduction • Mitigation of operational risks • Reputation • Licence to operate • Stakeholder recognition	• Reduction of gas flares • Reduction of oil spills and blowout • Preservation of biodiversity • Green Products • Containment of Water consumption (Reinjection and Water reuse) • Energy efficiency

The integration of DAPHNE's strategies with sustainability initiatives found its establishment in the 2014 integrated report. For the first time since its publication, DAPHNE's integrated report was aimed at explaining how the main strategic objectives were affected by the different capitals involved in the value chain by identifying the main initiatives that contribute to their achievement. A table illustrates the correlation between the main strategies from the upstream to the downstream (columns) and the key capitals that affect the organizational ability to create sustainable value (rows). Also, the report lists the key performance indicators of each capital in a table, classifying them according to the main strategies of the segments of the value chain. The indicators are analysed for a period of three years.

The principle-based approach suggested by the framework of the IIRC helped DAPHNE's reporting process evolve over the years, enabling the company to better understand its approach to sustainable value creation and how it affects the company's main strategic objectives. In particular, the integrated reporting process provided managers with a useful "box" in which to store the different performance information and capitals that influence the capacity to create sustainable value over the long term.

Although the reports for 2013 and 2014 were better structured and more oriented to the integration of financial and non-financial performance in order to achieve the company's strategic objectives, the two reports do not explain the correlations and interdependencies between sustainability initiatives and traditional business activities. In 2013 and 2014, it was still not very clear how sustainability and financial performance affect the value creation process and the main activities of the organization's value chain. Financial and non-financial capital were illustrated in the report, providing an inventory of information, without, however, delving into the analysis of its cause-effect relationship on the company's strategic objectives (see Figure 6.11).

Figure 6.11 – Correlations between DAPHNE's strategies and capitals (Source adapted from DAPHNE's integrated report, 2014)

	Cash Flow and Value Generation			
Strategic objectives/ Capitals	increase the value of explorative resources growth in upstream cash generation	return to structural profitability in the gas & power business	Turnaround in refining & marketing and Chemical businesses	Focus on efficiency
Financial Capital	• Investment selectivity • Reduction of opex per barrel • Reduction of exposure to partners/National Companies • Reduction of time-to-market	• Gas contracts portfolio restructuring • Working capital optimization • Simplifying the operations and optimization of logistic costs	• Investment selectivity • Opex reduction • Working capital optimization	• Capex reduction • G&A costs reduction • Working capital optimization
Productive Capital	• Exploration portfolio renewal • HPC computing Center • Proprietary instruments for seismic activity • Operatorship • Project execution optimization • Asset integrity	• Continental hub monitoring • Enhanced of Asset Back Trading • Upstream integration • Power plant optimization	• Critical sites reconversion/rationalization • Promotion of energy efficiency	• Process optimization • Lean Organization
Intellectual Capital	• R&S investments • Proprietary technologies development and patents management • Development of technologies to increase the recovery rate	• Take-or-pay risk integrated management • Development of innovative products and services • Evolution in processes and systems	• R&S investments • Business innovation • Research applied in green business	• Proprietary technologies development and patent management • Continuous improvement • Change management
Human Capital	• Safety in the workplace • Recruitment, education and training on the job • Internal know-how enhancement • Promotion of human rights • Knowledge management	• Safety in the workplace • Reorganization/streamlining operations • Internal know-how enhancement • Change management	• Safety in the workplace • Internal know-how enhancement • Internal mobility • Development of new skills	• Safety in the workplace • Involvement of employees • Internal know-how enhancement
Social and Relationship Capital	• Partnerships with governments and local authorities • Territorial development and Local content projects • Increase in access to energy • Respect of human rights • Promotion of transparency	• Gas advocacy • Relationship with customers and suppliers • Know-how in negotiations	• Trade union dialogue • Local stakeholder management • Strategic partnerships	• Trade union dialogue • Stakeholders management
Natural Capital	• Increase in oil&gas reserves • Oil spill reduction • Blowout reduction through optimization of upstream operations • Gas enhancement for zero gas flaring • Biodiversity protection and sensible areas	• Energy efficiency initiatives • Promotion to customers of energy efficiency	• Investments in biorefining and green chemistry • Promotion of energy efficiency	• Promotion of energy efficiency • Efficient use of resources

A first attempt to address the connectivity between financial and non-financial performance was made between 2015 and 2016 when the report showed a connectivity map for the first time. The connectivity map represented the outcome of a project for integrated reporting that started in 2013 and was launched by the Sustainability Unit to better illustrate how the company's sustainability initiatives and performance affect the long-term financial viability of the business (see Figure 6.12).

The connectivity map graphically illustrates the cause-effect connections among actions and initiatives taken in the upstream segment of the value chain to achieve the main strategic objectives, (i.e. fuel value and increase explorative resources, growth in upstream cash generation), and to respond to DAPHNE's external challenges. Further, the map shows the effects that these initiatives may have on the achievement of positive financial performance for the year, in comparison with future targets (i.e. connecting arrows). Also, it identifies the risks that may inhibit the achievement of DAPHNE's short, medium and long-term strategic objectives and the main performance for the year.

Coherent with the previous reporting years, the 2015 integrated report illustrates the main challenges that the company faces and the actions it must take to achieve the objectives of the following four-year plan. Also, the risk management process is described, analysing the top risks for the year and the actions taken to mitigate their impacts. The development of the connectivity map required the active participation of multiple managers in order to better highlight how sustainability initiatives affect the company's sustainable value creation process over the long-term. Also, the development of the connectivity map and more broadly of integrated reporting within DAPHNE had relevant effects on the organization decision making process.

Figure 6.12 – DAPHNE's connectivity map (Source adapted from DAPHNE's integrated report, 2015 p. 20)

To summarise the third phase of reporting within DAPHNE, the chart below briefly illustrates the changes in DAPHNE's approach to sustainability from 2010 to 2015 according to the contextual initiatives that took place in that period; the nature of the report produced; the key practices used and the units responsible for the preparation of the report (see Figure 6.13).

Figure 6.13 – The evolution of the meaning of sustainability, from 2010 to 2015

The evolution of sustainability reporting in DAPHNE	From 2010 to 2015		
External contingencies	• Improved National standards and guidelines on voluntary reporting • Climate change • Competitors' environmental disasters • The advent of the International Integrated Reporting Council		
Meanings of Sustainability	**2011-2012:** Sustainability as integrated within company's strategies. However, financial and sustainability performance are still separated. Collage of information	**2013-2014:** Sustainability as integrating multiple capitals (financial, manufacturing, uman, intellectual, social and relationship and natural) but classified as an inventory of information.	**2015:** Sustainability as integrated within the company business strategies connecting financial and non financial performance.
Report	Integrated report		
Key practices used	• Financial and non-financial performance • Integrated Business Model • Integrated Risk management Process • 4 year Strategic plan	• Capitals • Integrated Business Model • Integrated Risk management Process • 4 year Strategic plan • Materiality assessment	• Capitals • Integrated Business Model • Connectivity Map • Integrated Risk management Process • 4 year Strategic plan • Materiality assessment
Unit responsible for the preparation of the report	Sustainability Unit with the support of a workgroup composed of different managers from corporate planning, sustainability, external relations, corporate governance, and integrated risk management		Sustainability and Financial Unit with the support of the working group

6.5. Twenty years of sustainability reporting within DAPHNE and its effect on the organisation's strategies

This chapter provides an in-depth analysis of the dynamics and contingencies through which the meaning of sustainability emerged and evolved within DAPHNE, additionally due to the accounting and reporting practices used to represent it.

In particular, this chapter analyses the sustainability reporting process within DAPHNE from 1996 to 2015, defining three reporting phases and describing for each of them the primary external contingencies that influenced the adoption of the reports, the meaning of sustainability associated to them, the key practices used and the units responsible for the preparation of the report.

The analysis of the first reporting phase (1994-2005) shows how sustainability was interpreted mainly as an environmental concept that was disconnected from traditional business objectives and focused on reducing pollution by adopting renewable energy sources.

The privatization process started in the early nineties, including the need to improve the company's reputation and competitiveness in the market by expanding its external and internal communication process, thus improving the company's approach to sustainability including issues related to the health and safety of employees. The integration and monitoring of health and safety performance required DAPHNE to develop an *ad-hoc* performance measurement system that was able to collect and monitor non-financial performance.

New responsibility centres were established, such as the HSE department and the Corporate Social Responsibility Unit to facilitate the collaboration among different departments and to identify the sustainability initiatives that most influence the reputation of the company. As a result, the establishment of the new centre of responsibilities and the adoption of the HSE management accounting system contributed to give higher significance and relevance to sustainability issues influencing managers' actions and responsibilities.

However, the performance reported on the initiatives for the health and safety of employees and environmental development were still separate from each other and not even linked to the company's traditional activities. Sustainability as a concept was rarely mentioned and mainly referred to the idea of environmental development.

Sustainability gained further meaning in 2003 when the definition of Corporate Social Responsibility emerged. The concepts of sustainability and corporate social responsibility were often used interchangeably as synonymous, giving higher emphasis to the health and safety of employees and the social and economic development of the communities in which DAPHNE was operating at that time.

The analysis of the second phase of sustainability reporting focuses on the process of formalisation of sustainability in the company between 2006 and 2009. The structure of the reports changed in order to focus more on the future trends and challenges of the markets and the actions to be taken to mitigate risks and create opportunities. The adoption of the health and safety management system at the group level and its restructuring into an integrated management system that supported the sustainability reporting process within DAPHNE, contributed to share a meaning of sustainability that combined social and environmental development with stakeholder engagement.

In 2006, the establishment of the Sustainability Unit contributed to making the meaning of sustainability more established within company management and reporting practices. The development of internal workshops (i.e. the "leadership and sustainability" workshop) and the presentation of the sustainability business model were pursued to stimulate questioning among managers about the ethical component of usual managerial decisions and to create awareness of the existing connections between sustainability, decision-making processes and managerial action. However, sustainability as a concept was still perceived as being separate from the company's business strategies.

Sustainability developed further meaning within the company's evolving reporting phase between 2010 and 2015, when DAPHNE started a process of reconceptualization of sustainability initiatives, integrating them within the main business strategies to determine how environmental, social and economic initiatives affect the company's value creation process in the long run. During this third reporting phase, beginning in 2010, however, the adoption of integrated reporting further highlighted the discrepancies between financial and sustainability performance, in the process of illustrating the correlations between them.

Although attempting to summarise in one single report how multiple capitals and initiatives influence the ability of the organization to create sustainable value in the long term, DAPHNE's integrated reports were not able to communicate sustainability as a core aspect of the business without explaining whether and how sustainability and financial performance affect each other. An initial list of financial and non-financial performances related to the different capitals that affect the organization's capacity to create value is provided in the 2013 report. The same performances have been classified in 2014 according to the main strategic objectives to be achieved through the company's value chain. However, information reported between 2011 and 2014 still seemed disconnected, providing only a list (or an inventory) of data, which, although being gathered within the same reports, does not illustrate any connection. It was not very clear how sustainability initiatives and performance influenced and affected the reputation of the company, as well as the viability of the business in the long term.

The first connection of the multiple financial and non-financial performances that drive the achievement of specific organizational strategies can be found in 2015 when the connectivity map was published. The development of the connectivity map through integrated reporting had relevant effects on the decision-making process of the company. Further, the development of the connectivity map and the identification of the main capitals that affect the company's value creation process have been fundamental to determine the conversion of a traditional refinery into a bio-refinery in northern Italy.

The following chart synthesises the evolution of sustainability reporting and the meaning of sustainability, the key practices adopted and the unit responsible for its preparation from 1996 to 2015 (see Figure 6.15).

Figure 6.14 – The evolution of DAPHNE's sustainability reporting process from 1996 to 2015

<table>
<tr><th>The evolution of sustainability reporting in DAPHNE</th><th colspan="3">From 1996 to 2005</th><th>From 2006 to 2009</th><th colspan="3">From 2010 to 2015</th></tr>
<tr><td>External contingencies</td><td>• Globalization and internationalization of Oil and Gas companies
• Privatization process of the company from 1996 to 2001</td><td colspan="2">• Rio + 10, UN Earth Summit in Johannesburg, 2002
• Introduction of international regulations and guidelines on Corporate Social Responsibility (i.e. GRI and Global Compact)</td><td>• evolution of laws and regulations, both domestically and internationally
• International stakeholders pressure for higher transparency.</td><td colspan="3">• Improved National standards and guidelines on voluntary reporting
• Climate change
• Competitors' environmental disasters
• The advent of the International Integrated Reporting Council</td></tr>
<tr><td>Meanings of Sustainability</td><td colspan="2">1996-2002: Sustainability as combining environmental and Health and Safety issues disconnected from traditional business objectives</td><td>2003-2005: Sustainability as Corporate Social Responsibility, introducing the importance of stakeholders' engagement</td><td>2006-2009: Sustainability does not make distinctions between Environmental and social issues. Sustainability gives name to the report.</td><td>2011-2012: Sustainability as integrated within company's strategies. However, financial and sustainability performance are still separated. Collage of information</td><td>2013-2014: Sustainability as integrating multiple capitals (financial, manufacturing, uman, intellectual, social and relationship and natural) but classified as an inventory of information.</td><td>2015: Sustainability as integrated within the company business strategies connecting financial and non financial performance.</td></tr>
<tr><td>Report</td><td colspan="2">Health and safety and Environmental report</td><td>Corporate Social Responsibility Report</td><td>Sustainability Report</td><td colspan="3">Integrated report</td></tr>
<tr><td>Key practices used</td><td colspan="3">HSE Management System</td><td>• Model of Sustainability
• Integrated Management Sustainability process
• Materiality assessment process</td><td>• Financial and non-financial performance
• Integrated Business Model
• Integrated Risk management Process
• 4 year Strategic plan</td><td>• Capitals
• Integrated Business Model
• Integrated Risk management Process
• 4 year Strategic plan
• Materiality assessment</td><td>• Capitals
• Integrated Business Model
• Connectivity Map
• Integrated Risk management Process
• 4 year Strategic plan
• Materiality assessment</td></tr>
<tr><td>Unit responsible for the preparation of the report</td><td></td><td>• HSE Department in 2001</td><td>• CSR unit in 2003</td><td>Sustainability Unit</td><td colspan="2">Sustainability Unit with the support of a workgroup composed of different managers from corporate planning, sustainability, external relations, corporate governance, and integrated risk management.</td><td>Sustainability and Financial Unit with the support of the working group</td></tr>
</table>

6.6. The role of corporate and integrated reporting as organizations attempt to represent sustainability

As suggested earlier in this study, whereas the literature has discussed the representational ability of sustainability and integrated reports, maintaining that a gap still exists between "what companies say" and "what they do" about sustainability, this study argues that the attempt to represent this concept, and give it meaning, through incomplete accounting practices may produce valuable effects. Therefore, rather than trying to address this gap and offer guidelines to fully define sustainability, this study explores how organizations' attempts to represent sustainability (i.e. its represent*ing* – the process of representation) affect the way in which organizations understand and report on sustainability, changing its meaning over time.

How is the concept of sustainability represented through accounting and reporting practices?

The key point addressed in this study refers to the need to explore the space between accounting as a means of representation and construction of realities. Accounting for sustainability, with its ambiguities, inconsistencies and lack of a legitimate, unified corpus of knowledge and practices, is an interesting *locus*[12] to explore how accounting prospers exactly because of these ambiguities and inconsistencies (Christensen *et al.*, 2013). These allow accounting to emerge, proliferate and change over time (Meyer, 1986). When faced with the complexities of accounting for a multiple and heterogeneous variety of stakeholders, the incompleteness of accounting is magnified to a state that cannot be hidden by a faith in the power of its representations or in its power of reality making. Ambiguities (and not facts) cannot be ignored or reduced and are therefore to be embraced (Quattrone, 2017).

In doing so, accounting and reporting practices offer a number of representations (graphs, diagrams, tables, grid) that have generative power.

Figure 6.10 and 6.11 help making the point. How do these two figures represent sustainability? They do so by juxtaposing values – in the form of multiple capitals – that cannot be made homogeneous but still force preparers and users to search for a compromise. They expose an inner tension between, for instance, financial and natural matters, provoking the readers to speculate on those tensions. Although this may well be in the intention of the prepares of this document, the way data are put 'in form' to become information available to stakeholders cannot work as an 'answer machine'

---

[12] From Latin: the place where something is situated or occurs. A center of Activity

for there are no obvious answers in this document of how to reconcile business and environment. However, the report creates room for speculation and mediation that is open to multiple interpretations. This is also the case for Figure 6.12 where the logical flow presented by the designer of the reports requires readers to address a series of choices (like in labyrinths where one faces a wall and is forced to reflect on whether to go right or left, Carruthers, 1990). Thus, the inconsistencies and incomplete spaces that integrated reporting leaves, are those that attract the users by giving them an active role. The user is no longer a spectator but an integral part of the process. Notably, this process is possible because accounting and reporting practices, and in this particular case integrated reporting, contribute to generate a discursive space between multiple and diverse interpretations of sustainability. This discursive space facilitates the construction and reconstruction of the meaning of sustainability.

In this way, the generative power and incompleteness of accounting representations are the mechanisms that sustain the unfolding search for 'sustainable value' (see Figures 6.7; 6.8 and 6.9) that organizational discourses entail, and that make integrated reporting a viable practice. Therefore, this study maintains that it is not in the enlargement of the realm of the measurable (from one to several capitals) that the power of accounting lies, but in the mechanisms of juxtaposing these heterogeneous capitals in a clear reporting format. Further, this study maintains that accounting can never tell the truth, it can never work as an answering machine (Burchell *et al.*, 1980) and we never find ourselves free from uncertainties and ambiguities (Revellino and Mouritsen, 2015). Instead, accounting and reporting can work as a 'maieutic machine' (Quattrone, 2015; Busco and Quattrone, 2017) which can force a community to ask questions with the never fulfilled promise of a compromise.

6.7. Summary and some further thoughts

What is meant to be sustainable for a business? And how do sustainability initiatives and performance affect the organization's ability to create value in the long run?

As Gray (2010) suggested, these questions probably have no answer and cannot be answered at the organizational level. It is suggested that organizations communicate to external stakeholders how they contribute to sustainable development through their reporting process, by explaining how and whether they are able to create or destroy value for the community in which they operate. However, sustainability reporting and, more recently, integrated reporting are often implemented for legitimacy purposes without explaining whether the information reported reflects the actions taken by the company towards sustainable development (Milne and Gray, 2013; Van Bommel, 2014; Higgins *et al.* 2014; Zappettini and Unerman, 2016).

As illustrated in Chapter Three, sustainability accounting and reporting practices cannot provide complete representations of what an organization does to be sustainable (Gond, 2009; Gray, 2010; 2006). Accounting and reporting practices are intrinsically incomplete and are not able to provide answers regarding what is meant to be sustainable for a business (Busco and Quattrone, 2014; Quattrone, 2015). On the contrary, they help to envision corporate financial and sustainable challenges and goals, shaping how users perceive, understand and relate to sustainability (Quattrone, 2009; 2015).

As described in this chapter, the implementation of multiple approaches to sustainability reporting over time, as well as the practices and routines adopted to manage multiple performances and perspectives (Contrafatto and Burns, 2013), all contributed to the evolution of what sustainability meant as it was integrated into the business.

This chapter illustrates that sustainability and, in particular integrated reports, provided users with a "space" through which the meaning of sustainability and the significance of its determinants were reconsidered and reinforced according to the company's principal strategies (Contrafatto, 2014).

The production of texts as organizational "discursive objects" (Hardy *et al.* 2000), such as those produced by the HSE, sustainability and integrated reports have contributed to "make" sustainability a "discursive concept" that is recognizable and operable in practice, and that is continually gaining meaning within the company's principal strategies because of the involvement of different actors in their development (Miller and Napier, 1993, p. 641).

Chapter 7
CONCLUSIONS

SUMMARY: 7.1. Contributions to the research. – 7.2. Suggestions for further research and empirical implications.

This book explored the role of corporate and integrated reporting as organizations attempt to represent sustainability.

Several studies have criticised accounting and reporting practices for having offered limited representations of the ways in which organizations operate to be sustainable (Gray, 2010; Tregidga *et al.* 2014), and for their failure to fill the gap between what companies say and what they actually do about sustainability (Higgins *et al.* 2014).

Although these practices are not able to provide faithful and complete representations of organizations' initiatives and performance regarding sustainability (Gond *et al.*, 2009; Gray, 2010; 2006), they have the potential to envision corporate financial and sustainability challenges, and thus affect how users perceive, understand and relate to sustainability (Quattrone, 2009; 2015).

While much is known about the ways in which organizations represent their performance and initiatives on sustainability (see Livesey, 2001; 2002; Milne *et al.* 2006; Laine, 2009; and Tregidga and Milne, 2006), much less is known about how sustainability gains meaning and is constructed through organizations accounting and reporting practices (Tregidga *et al.* 2012; Cho *et al.* 2015; O'Dwyer and Unerman, 2016).

This book combined theoretical and empirical insights to show that accounting and reporting practices (and in this particular case integrated reporting) are not relevant for the way in which they reflect organizations activities and performance towards sustainability. On the contrary, corporate and integrated reporting practices provide the condition for "sustainability" (as a discursive concept) to be filled with an ever-unfolding meaning.

7.1. Contributions to the research

This study offers a number of contributions. First, it adds to the literature on sustainability accounting and reporting practices by showing that these practices are not expected to offer complete representations or to provide "answers" to organizations on how to be sustainable. Rather, this study maintains that accounting and reporting practices offer a number of representations (graphs, diagrams, tables, grid) that have generative power. In doing so, accounting and reporting representations affect the way in which organizations understand and report about sustainability, changing its meaning over time.

The meaning of sustainability within DAPHNE's sustainability and integrated reports evolved in accordance with the practices used to represent it. The lack of definition of sustainability and the multiple interpretations attached to this concept, together with the incompleteness of accounting representations provided users with a space for interaction that helped managers to define, understand, debate and reflect on the organizational initiatives that affect the long-term sustainability of the business.

Importantly, this study demonstrates that sustainability can never be fully fixed (i.e. it is always contingent, as seen in Gray, 2010) and as such it could always take on different meanings. Thus, the "open ended" nature of the concept of sustainability (see for example Frame and O'Connor, 2011; Tregidga *et al.* 2011, 2012, 2014), as well as the incapacity of accounting and reporting practices to provide complete representations (see for example, Hines, 1988; Morgan, 1988; Shapiro, 1997; Mattessich, 2003; Messner, 2009; Jordan and Messner; 2012) of an organization's activities towards sustainability, offer opportunities to 'talk about it' in several ways, thereby, providing the potential to stimulate debate among different perspectives. Here, the generative power and incompleteness of accounting representations are the mechanisms that sustain the unfolding search for 'sustainable value' that organizational discourses entail, and that make integrated reporting a viable practice. This discursive space facilitates the construction and reconstruction of the meaning of sustainability throughout the represent*ing* process.

In doing so, accounting and reporting practices unfold themselves, and evolve, as a consequence of the debate about sustainability that this process produces, changing the subject positions that are involved in it.

Since these practices are attached to unfolding meanings of sustainability and become discursive objects, they unfold themselves through the process of stimulating further discourse about sustainability, changing the subject positions that were involved in the company reporting process.

In this regard, rather than trying to fill 'sustainability' with stable meanings, this study explores the mechanisms for making *it* meaning*ful*, and considers the role played by practices such as sustainability and integrated reporting within these mechanisms.

The next section addresses the main limitations of this research together with opportunities for future research.

7.2. Suggestions for further research and empirical implications

The findings of this study have implications for further research into the role of accounting and reporting practices for sustainability. If accounting and reporting practices stimulate discussion into what is sustainable for an organization, it is important to understand not only how these practices engage their users, but also how this engagement makes an undefined concept such as sustainability unfold due to the different perspectives that accounting and reporting practices bring to light.

New studies are needed to determine how sustainability is brought into practice in the ongoing attempt to represent it throughout the reporting process, exploring ways in which the various actors within organizations interact throughout the reporting process in order to understand how sustainability initiatives affect the overall strategic approach of an organization.

Further studies are needed to explain the role of accounting and reporting in engaging multiple actors in questioning and debating what it means to be sustainable within different types of settings, ranging from small and medium-sized enterprises to global organizations.

This research also suggests opportunities for further exploration into how evolving conceptions of sustainability may be 'objectified', that is, moulded into different material practices and discursive objects within organizations, such as company performance measurement, management control, and IT systems (e.g. ERP or business intelligence systems). Although this research concentrates on accounting and reporting practices as the main discursive objects possessing receptivity within DAPHNE, other practices or tools in different settings could be associated with different conceptions of sustainability. Analysis of alternative media, which contribute to integrate sustainability initiatives and performance, would be beneficial. It would be interesting to explore how sustainability objectives are integrated into a company's strategic planning, by explaining how they are operationalized in practice (see O'Dwyer and Unerman, 2016).

Making sustainability meaningful within an organization's strategies also means involving company stakeholders in the decision-making process. Accounting and reporting practices, as engagement platforms, can go beyond the representation of sustainability initiatives through a set of ad hoc targets and key performance indicators to include processes of engagement among the different stakeholders involved.

It would be relevant to understand the level of stakeholder engagement in making sustainability meaningful through company accounting and reporting practices, exploring how they contribute to increasing stakeholder pervasiveness and engagement in the decision-making process.

This aspect may have implications for the accounting profession as it may suggest ways for redesigning the role of management accountants in managing financial and non-financial information towards sustainable value creation. In particular, changes in the way in which sustainability is perceived within organizations may affect not only accounting and reporting practices and their use, but also the role of accountants in their development (Busco *et al.*, 2013a). In this regard, future research would be useful to explore the role that management accountants may play in leading to the integration of sustainability initiatives and performance within organizations.

Management accountants and finance experts, in general, can have a central role within organizations by suggesting accounting practices and performance measurement systems that are able to monitor and communicate how business objectives affect the value created or destroyed for a multitude of stakeholders. The finance unit can take the centre stage in this process, acting as both architect and orchestrator of a process of thinking, measuring and reporting that mediates among multiple concerns, facilitates conversations and fosters the generation of innovative solutions within contexts that are characterized by multiple backgrounds and points of view.

Future research is required to compare how sustainability discourse is constructed within multiple organizations, investigating how managers are involved in this process. In the case study analysed in this research, the concept of sustainability gained multiple and conflicting meanings within the same organization, and therefore, it is expected to assume different interpretations by also looking at different business models and sectors.

Accordingly, as suggested by O'Dwyer and Unerman (2016), greater attention should be given to the study of reporting and decision-making for Sustainable Development Goals, as well as to the techniques used in ethical businesses such as "B Corporations". Here there is the potential to open up unique, new examples of 'accounting for social sustainability in action', particularly where organizational logics are likely to collide, as well as guiding future reporting developments in accounting for sustainability in conventional corporations.

Finally, considering the increasing number of regulations and standards issued for sustainability and integrated reporting (e.g. GRI, Global Compact, IIRC, SASB), as well as the recent approval of EU directive 2014/195, it would be relevant to explore how these regulations influence the meaning of sustainability and affect the company reporting process because of the compliance that these regulations and directives require.

REFERENCES

Adams C.A. (2004), "The ethical, social and environmental reporting – performance portrayal gap", *Accounting, Auditing and Accountability Journal*, Vol. 17 No. 5, pp. 731-757.

Adams C.A., (2014), "The international integrated reporting council: a call to action", *Critical Perspectives on Accounting*, Vol. 27, pp. 23-28.

Adams C.A. and Larrinaga-González C. (2007), "Engaging with organisations in pursuit of improved sustainability accounting and performance", *Accounting, Auditing & Accountability Journal*, Vol. 20 No. 3, pp. 333-355.

Adams C.A. and McNicholas P. (2007), "Making a difference: Sustainability reporting, accountability and organisational change", *Accounting, Auditing and Accountability Journal*, Vol. 20 No. 3, pp. 382-402.

Ahrens T., (1997), "Talking accounting: an ethnography of management knowledge in British and German brewers", *Accounting, Organisations and Society*, Vol. 22 No. 7, pp. 617-637.

Ahrens T. and Chapman. C. (2007), "Management accounting as practice". *Accounting, Organizations and Society*, Vol. 32 No. 1-2, pp. 1-27.

Alvesson M. and Karreman D. (2000), "Varieties of discourse: On the study of organizations through discourse analysis", *Human Relations*, Vol. 53 No. 9, pp. 1125-1149.

Anderson-Gough F., Grey C. and Robson K. (2000), "In the name of the client: The service ethic in two professional services firms", *Human Relations*, Vol. 53, pp. 1151-1174.

Andon P., Baxter J. and Chua W.F. (2007), "Accounting change as relational drifting: A field study of experiments with performance measurement", *Management Accounting Research*, Vol. 18, pp. 273-308

Aras G. and Crowther D. (2009), "Corporate Sustainability Reporting: A Study in Disingenuity?", *Journal of Business Ethics*, Vol. 87 No. S1, pp. 279-288.

Archel P., Husillos J. and Spence C. (2011), "The institutionalisation of unaccountability: Loading the dice of Corporate Social Responsibility discourse", *Accounting, Organizations and Society*, Vol. 36 No. 6, pp. 327-343.

Austin J.L. (1962), *How to do Things with Words*. Oxford: Oxford University Press.

Bayou M.E., Reinstein A. and Williams F.P. (2011), "To tell the truth: A discussion of issues concerning truth and ethics in accounting", *Accounting Organization and Society*, Vol. 36, pp. 109-124.

Bebbington J. (2001), "Sustainable development: A review of the international development, business and accounting literature" *Accounting Forum*, Vol. 25 No. 2, pp. 128-157.

Bebbington J. (2009), "Measuring sustainable development performance: Possibilities and issues", *Accounting Forum,* Vol. 33 No. 3, pp. 189-193

Bebbington J. and Gray R. (2001), "An Account of Sustainability: Failure, Success and a Reconceptualization", *Critical Perspectives on Accounting*, Vol. 12 No. 5, pp. 557-588.

Bebbington J., Larrinaga-González C. and Moneva-Abadía J.M. (2008), "Legitimating reputation/the reputation of legitimacy theory", *Accounting, Auditing & Accountability Journal*, Vol. 21 No. 3, pp. 371-374.

Bebbington J., Brown J., Frame B. and Thomson I. (2007), "Theorizing engagement: the potential of a critical dialogic approach", *Accounting, Auditing & Accountability Journal,* Vol. 20 No. 3, pp. 356-381.

Bebbington J. and Larrinaga C. (2014), "Accounting and sustainable development: An exploration", *Accounting, Organisations and Society*, Vol. 39 No. 6, pp. 395-413.

Beech N. (2000), "Narrative styles of managers and workers: A tale of star-crossed lovers". *Journal of Applied Behavioral Science*, Vol. 53, pp. 210-218.

Berger P.L. and Luckmann T. (1967), *The Social Construction of Reality. A Treatise in the Sociology of Knowledge*, Garden City, NY: Doubleday, Anchor Books.

Berry A.J. and Otley D. (2004), "Case-based research in accounting". In C. Humphrey and B. Lee, *The real life guide to accounting research: a behind-the-scenes view of using qualitative research methods*, Oxford: Elsevier, pp. 231-255.

Boje D. M. (1995), "Stories of the Storytelling Organization: A postmodern analysis of Disney as 'Tamara-Land'". *Academy of Management Journal*, Vol. 38 No. 4, pp. 997-1035.

Bolzoni L. (1995), *La stanza della memoria. Modelli letterari e iconografici nell'età della stampa.* Einaudi, Turin (English Translation by Parzen J., *The Gallery of Memory: Literary and Iconographic Models in the Age of the Printing Press*, University of Toronto Press, Toronto).

Brown J. and Dillard J., (2014), "Integrated reporting: On the need for broadening out and opening up", *Accounting, Auditing & Accountability Journal*, Vol. 27 No. 7, pp. 1120-1156.

Burchell S., Clubb C., Hopwood A., Hughes S., Nahapiet J. (1980). "The roles of accounting in organizations and society", *Accounting, Organization and Society.* Vol. 5 No.1.

Burritt R. and Schaltegger S. (2010), "Sustainability accounting and reporting: fad or trend?" *Accounting, Auditing and Accountability Journal*, Vol. 23 No. 7, pp. 829-846.

Busco C., Riccaboni A. and Scapens R.W. (2006), Trust for accounting and accounting for trust, *Management Accounting Research*, Vol. 17 No. 1, pp. 11-41.

Busco C., Quattrone P. (2015), "Exploring how the balanced scorecard engages and unfolds: Articulating the visual power of accounting inscriptions", *Contemporary Accounting Research*, Vol. 32 No. 3, pp. 1236-1262.

Busco C., Frigo M.L., Quattrone P. and Riccaboni A. (2013a), *Towards integrated reporting: concepts, elements and principles*, Springer, London, UK.

Busco C., Frigo M.L., Quattrone P. and Riccaboni A. (2013b), "Redefining corporate accountability through integrated reporting: What happens when values and value creation meet?", *Strategic Finance* Vol. 95 No. 2, pp. 33-42.

Busco C., Granà F. and Izzo M.F. (2018), *Sustainable Development Goals and Integrated Reporting,* Routledge and Giappichelli, New York, USA.

Busco C. and Quattrone P. (2017) "In Search of the "Perfect One": How accounting as a maieutic machine sustains inventions through generative 'in-tensions'". *Management Accounting Research*, (*in press*).

Butler J. (2005). *Giving an account of oneself*. New York: Fordham University Press.

Carruthers M., (1990), *The book of memory: A study of memory in medieval culture*, Cambridge University Press, New York.

Carruthers M., (1998), *The craft of thought: Meditation, rhetoric, and the making of images. 400–1200*, Cambridge University Press, Cambridge.

Chapman C. (1997), "Reflections on a Contingent View of Accounting," *Accounting Organizations and Society*, Vol. 22 No. 2, pp. 189-205.

Chapman R. and Milne M.J. (2003), "The triple bottom line: how New Zealand companies measure up Corporate Strategy", *International Journal for Sustainable Business*, Vol. 11 No. 2, pp. 37-50.

Chenhall R.H., Hall M. and Smith D. (2013), "Performance measurement, modes of evaluation and the development of compromising accounts", *Accounting, Organizations and Society*, Vol. 38 No. 4, pp. 268-287.

Chia R. (2000), "Discourse Analysis as Organisational Analysis", *Organization*, Vol. 7 No. 3, pp. 513-518.

Cho C.H., Roberts R.W. and Patten D.M. (2010), "The language of US corporate environmental disclosure", *Accounting, Organizations and Society*, Vol. 35 No. 4, pp. 431-443.

Cho C.H., Laine M., Roberts R.W. and Rodrigue M. (2015), "Organized hypocrisy, organizational façades, and sustainability reporting", *Accounting, Organizations and Society*, Vol. 40, pp. 78-94.

Christensen L.T., Morsing M. and Thyssen O. (2013), "CSR as aspirational talk", *Organization*, Vol. 20 No. 3, pp. 372-393.

Christensen L.T., Morsing M. and Thyssen O. (2015a), "Discursive Closure and Discursive Openings in Sustainability", *Management Communication Quarterly*, Vol. 29 No. 1, pp. 135-144.

Christensen L.T., Morsing M. and Thyssen O. (2015b), "The polyphony of values and the value of polyphony", *Journal for Communication Studies*, Vol. 8 No 1(15), pp. 9-25.

Cohen M., March G.J. and Olsen J. (1972), "A Garbage Can Model of Organization Choice", *Administrative Science Quarterly*, Vol. 17 No. 1, pp. 1-25.

Cohen S., Demeritt D., Robinson J. and Rothman D. (1998), "Climate Change and Sustainable Development: Towards Dialogue", *Global Environmental Change*, Vol. 8 No. 4, pp. 341-71.

Contrafatto M. (2014), "The institutionalization of social and environmental reporting: An Italian narrative", *Accounting, Organizations and Society*, Vol. 39 No. 6, pp. 414-432.

Contrafatto M. and Burns J. (2013), "Social and environmental accounting, organizational change and management accounting: A processual view", *Management Accounting Research*, Vol. 24 No. 4, pp. 349-365.

Cooper D.J., Hayes D. and Wolf F. (1981), "Accounting in organized anarchies: Understanding and designing accounting systems in ambiguous situations". *Accounting, Organizations and Society*, Vol. 6 No. 3, pp. 175-191.

Czarniawska B., (1997), *Narrating the organization: Dramas of institutional identity,* Chicago University Press, Chicago.

Czarniawska B. (1998), *A Narrative approach to organization studies*, SAGE University Paper, SAGE, Thousand Oaks, London, New Delhi.

de Villiers C., Rinaldi L., Unerman J., (2014), "Integrated Reporting: Insights, gaps and an agenda for future research", *Accounting, Auditing & Accountability Journal*, Vol. 27 No. 7, pp. 1042-1067.

Dey C. and Burns J. (2010), Integrated Reporting at a Novo Nordisk. In: Hopwood A., Unerman J., Fries J. (ed.), *Accounting for Sustainability: Practical Insights*, Oxford: Earthscan, pp. 215-232.

Dick P. (2004), "Discourse analysis", in Cassell C. and Symon G. (eds), *Essential Guide to Qualitative Methods and Analysis in Organizational Research*, SAGE Publications Ltd, London, UK, pp. 203-213.

Drexhage J., Murphy D. (2010), *Sustainable development: from Brundtland to Rio 2012, Background paper for the high level panel on global sustainability*, United Nations, New York, pp.1-26.

Drew P. and Sorjonen M.-L. (1997), "Institutional dialogue". In T.A. Van Dijk (ed.), *Discourse studies: A multidisciplinary introduction*. Vol. 2: Discourse as Social Interaction. SAGE Publications Ltd, London, UK. pp. 92-119.

Dunford R. and Jones D. (2000), "Narrative in strategic change", *Human Relations* Vol. 53, pp. 1207-1226.

Dumay J., Bernardi C., Guthrie J., Demartini P., (2016), "Integrated reporting: A structured literature review", *Accounting Forum*, Vol. 40 No. 3, pp. 166-185.

Eccles R.G. and Krzus M.P., (2010). *One Report: Integrated Reporting for a Sustainable* Strategy, John Wiley & Sons, Hoboken, NJ.

Eccles R.G. and Serafeim G. (2013), "The performance frontier", *Harvard business review,* Vol. 91 No. 5, pp. 50-60.

Eccles R.G. and Spiesshofer B. (2015), "Integrated Reporting for a Re-Imagined Capitalism", *Harvard Business Review*, Working Paper 16-032, pp. 1-24.

Elkington J. (1997), *Cannibals with forks: The Triple Bottom Line of 21st century*, Oxford: Capstone Publishing

European Commission (2014), *Disclosure of non-financial and diversity information by large companies and groups – Frequently asked questions*, Brussels.

Fairclough N. (1992), *Discourse and Social Change*, Polity Press, Cambridge, MA.

Flower J., (2015), "The International Integrated Reporting Council: a story of failure", *Critical Perspectives on Accounting*, Vol. 27, pp. 1-17.

Fairhurst G. and Putnam L. (2004), "Organizations as Discursive Constructions", *Communication Theory*, Vol. 14 No. 1, pp. 5-26.

Fairhurst G. and Cooren F. (2004), "Organizational Language in use: Interaction Analysis, Conversation Analysis and Speech Act Schematics", in Grant D., Hardy C., Oswick C. and Putnam L. (Eds), *The SAGE Handbook of Organizational Discourse,* SAGE Publications Ltd, London, UK, pp. 131-153.

Ferns G. and Amaeshi K. (2017), "Struggles at the Summits: Discourse Coalitions, Field Boundaries, and the Shifting Role of Business in Sustainable Development", *Business & Society,* pp. 1-39.

Foucault M. (1972), *The Archeology of Knowledge*, Pantheon Books, New York, NY.

Foucault M. (1977), "Truth and power". In C. Gordon (Ed.), *Power/knowledge: Selected interviews and other writings 1972-1977*, Sussex: Harvester Press, pp. 109-133.

Foucault M. (1978), *The History of Sexuality*, Volume 1: An Introduction. Harmondsworth: Penguin.

Foucault M. (1979). *Discipline and Punish: The Birth of the Prison*. Harmondsworth: Penguin.

Foucault M. (1980), *Power/Knowledge: Selected Interviews and Other Writings* 1972-1977. Brighton: Harvester Press.

Frame B. and O'Connor M. (2011), "Integrating valuation and deliberation: the purposes of sustainability assessment", *Environmental Science and Policy*, Vol. 14 No. 1, pp. 1-10.

Gibassier D., Rodrigue M. and Arjaliès D.L. (2016). "Integrated Reporting Is Like God – No One Has Met Him, but Everybody Talks about Him': The Power of Myth in the Adoption of an Innovation". SSRN working paper.

Giovannoni E. and Quattrone P. (2017), "The materiality of absence: Emptiness, institutions and the incomplete cathedral", *Organization Studies*, (forthcoming).

Gond J.P., Palazzo G. and Basu K. (2009), "Reconsidering instrumental corporate social responsibility through the Mafia metaphor" *Business Ethics Quarterly*, Vol. 19 No. 1, pp. 57-85.

Gond J.-P., Grubnic S., Herzig C. and Moon J. (2012). "Configuring management control systems: Theorizing the integration of strategy and sustainability", *Management Accounting Research*, Vol. 23 No. 3, pp. 205-223.

Grant D., Hardy C., Oswick C. and Putnam L. (2004), "Introduction: Organizational Discourse: Exploring the Field", in Grant D., Hardy C., Oswick C. and Putnam L. (Eds), *The SAGE Handbook of Organizational Discourse*, SAGE Publications Ltd, London, UK, pp. 1-36.

Global Reporting Initiative (GRI), (2013), *Reporting principles and standards disclosure*, pp. 1-93.

Gray R. (2002), "Of Messiness, Systems and Sustainability: Towards a more Social and Environmental Finance and Accounting", *British Accounting Review*, Vol. 34, pp. 357-386.

Gray R. (2006a), "Does sustainability reporting improve corporate behaviour?: Wrong question? Right time?" *Accounting and Business Research*, Vol. 36 No. sup1, pp. 65-88.

Gray R. (2006b), "Social, environmental and sustainability reporting and organisational value creation? Whose value? Whose creation?" *Accounting, Auditing & Accountability Journal*, Vol. 19 No. 6, pp. 793-819.

Gray R. (2010), "Is accounting for sustainability actually accounting for sustainability…and how would we know? An exploration of narratives of organisations and the planet", *Accounting, Organizations and Society*, Vol. 35 No. 1, pp. 47-62.

Gray R.H. and Bebbington K.J. (2001), *Accounting for the environment* (2nd ed.). SAGE Publications Ltd, London, UK.

Gray R. and Milne M. (2002), "Sustainability Reporting: Who's Kidding Whom?" *Chartered Accountants Journal of New Zealand*, Vol. 81 No .6, pp. 66-70.

Hajer M. (1995), *The politics of environmental discourse: Ecological modernization and the policy process*, Oxford: Oxford University Press.

Hall M. (2010) "Accounting information and managerial work", *Accounting, Organizations and Society*, Vol. 35 No. 3, pp. 301-315.

Han Onn A. and Woodley A. (2014), "A discourse analysis on how the sustainability agenda is defined within the mining industry", *Journal of Cleaner Production*, Vol. 84 No. 1, pp. 116-127.

Hardy C. (2004), "Scaling up and bearing down in discourse analysis: questions regarding textual agencies and their context", *Organization*, Vol. 11, pp. 415-425.

Hardy C. and Phillips (1999), "No joking matter: Discursive struggle in the Canadian refugee system". *Organization Studies*, Vol. 20, pp. 1-24.

Hardy C. and N. Phillips (2004), "Discourse and power". In D. Grant, C. Hardy, C. Oswick and L. Putnam (eds), *The Sage Handbook of Organizational Discourse*. SAGE Publications Ltd, London, UK.

Hardy C. and Thomas R. (2015), "Discourse in a Material World", *Journal of Management Studies,* Vol. 52 No. 5, pp. 680-696.

Hardy C., Lawrence T. and Phillips N. (1998), "Talking action: Conversations, narrative and action in interorganizational collaboration". In Grant D., Keenoy T.

and Oswick C. (Eds.), *Discourse and organization*. SAGE Publications Ltd, London, UK, pp. 65-83.

Hardy C., Palmer I. and Phillips N. (2000), "Discourse as a Strategic Resource", *Human Relations*, Vol. 53 No. 9, pp. 1227-1248.

Hardy C., Lawrence T.B. and Grant D. (2005), "Discourse and collaboration: the role of conversations and collective identity", *Academy of Management Review*, Vol. 30 No. 1, pp. 58-77.

Higgins C., Stubbs W. and Love T., (2014), "Walking the talk(s): Organisational narratives of integrated reporting", *Accounting, Auditing & Accountability Journal*, Vol. 27 No. 7, pp. 1090-1119.

Hines R.D. (1988), "Financial accounting: In communicating reality, we construct reality", *Accounting. Organizations and Society*, Vol. 13 No. 3, pp. 251-261.

Hopwood B., Mellor M. and O'Brien G. (2005), "Sustainable development: mapping different approaches", *Sustainable Development*, Vol. 13 No. 1, pp. 38-52.

Hopwood A.G. (2009), "Accounting and the environment", *Accounting, Organizations and Society*, Vol. 34 No. 3-4, pp. 433-439.

Humphrey C., O'Dwyer B. and Unerman, J. (2016), "Re-theorizing the configuration of organizational fields: the IIRC and the pursuit of 'Enlightened' corporate reporting", *Accounting and Business Research*, Vol. 47 No. 1, pp. 30-63.

ICSU, ISSC (2015): *Review of the Sustainable Development Goals: The Science Perspective*. Paris: International Council for Science (ICSU). ISBN: 978-0-930357-97-9.

International Integrated Reporting Council, (2013), *The International <IR> Framework*, IIRC.

IPIECA (2015), *Oil and gas industry guidance on voluntary sustainability reporting*, IPIECA, pp. 1-174.

Jordan S. and Messner M. (2012), "Enabling control and the problem of incomplete performance indicators", *Accounting, Organizations and Society*, Vol. 37, pp. 544-564.

Jørgensen B. and Messner M. (2010), "Accounting and strategising: A case study from new product development", *Accounting, Organizations and Society*, Vol. 35 No. 2, pp. 184-204.

Jorgensen M. and Phillips L.J. (2002), *Discourse Analysis as Theory and Method*, SAGE Publications Ltd, London, UK.

Joseph G. (2012), "Ambiguous but tethered: An accounting basis for sustainability reporting", *Critical Perspectives on Accounting*, Vol. 23 No. 2, pp. 93-106.

KPMG Advisory N.V. (2015). *Carrots & Sticks: Global trends in sustainability reporting regulation and policy*. pp. 1-96.

Laclau E. (2000), "Foreword", in Howarth D., Norval A. and Stavrakakis Y. (Eds.). *Discourse theory and political analysis: Identities, hegemonies and social change*, Manchester: Manchester University Press, pp. x-xi.

Laclau E. and Mouffe C. (1985), *Hegemony and socialist strategy: Towards a radical democratic politics.* (W Moore and P Cammack, Trans.) London: Verso.

Laine M. (2005), "Meanings of the term 'sustainable development' in Finnish corporate disclosures", *Accounting Forum*, Vol. 29 No. 4, pp. 395-413.

Laine M. (2009), "Ensuring legitimacy through rhetorical changes? A longitudinal interpretation of the environmental disclosures of a leading Finnish chemical company", *Accounting, Auditing and Accountability Journal*, Vol. 22 No. 7, pp. 1029-1054.

Latour B. (1987), *Science in Action. How to Follow Scientists and Engineers Through Society*. Cambridge Mass.: Harvard University Press.

Lillis, A.M. (2002), "Managing multiple dimensions of manufacturing performance – an exploratory study", *Accounting, Organizations and Society*,Vol. 27 No. 6,pp. 497-529.

Livesey S.M. (2001), "Eco-Identity as Discursive Struggle: Royal Dutch/Shell, Brent Spar and Nigeria", *Journal of Business Communication*, Vol. 38 No. 1, pp. 58-91.

Livesey S.M. (2002), "The Discourse of the Middle Ground: Citizen Shell Commits to Sustainable Development", *Management Communication Quarterly*, Vol. 15 No. 3, pp. 313-349.

DAPHNE, (2001), *Health, Safety and Environmental Report,* pp. 1-48.

DAPHNE, (2002), *Health, Safety and Environmental Report*, pp. 1-68.

DAPHNE, (2003), *Corporate Social Responsibility report*, pp. 1-84.

DAPHNE, (2006), *sustainability report*, pp. 1-109.

DAPHNE, (2007), *sustainability report*, pp. 1-92.

DAPHNE, (2008), *sustainability report*, pp. 1-91.

DAPHNE, (2009), *sustainability report,* pp. 1-100.

DAPHNE, (2010), *annual integrated report,* pp. 1-383.

DAPHNE, (2011), *annual integrated report,* pp. 1-391.

DAPHNE, (2012), *annual integrated report,* pp. 1-264.

DAPHNE, (2013), *annual integrated report,* pp. 1-273.

DAPHNE, (2014), *annual integrated report,* pp. 1-107.

DAPHNE, (2015), *annual integrated report,* pp. 1-106.

Lozano R. (2008), "Envisioning sustainability three-dimensionally", *Journal of Cleaner Production*, Vol. 16 No. 17, pp. 1838-1846.

Lozano R. and Huisingh D. (2011), "Inter-linking issues and dimensions in sustainability reporting", *Journal of Cleaner Production*, Vol. 19 No. 2-3, pp. 99-107.

Maguire S. and Hardy C. (2013), "Organizing processes and the construction of risk: A discursive approach", *Academy of Management Journal*, Vol. 56 No. 1, pp. 231-255.

Marshak R.J. and Grant D. (2008), "Organizational Discourse and New Organization Development Practices", *British Journal of Management*, Vol. 19, pp. S7-S19.

Mattessich R. (2003), "Accounting representation and the onion model of reality: A comparison with Baudrillard's orders of simulacra and his hyperreality", *Accounting, Organizations and Society*, Vol. 28, pp. 443-470.

Mauws M.K. (2000), "But is it art? Decision making and discursive resources in the field of cultural production", *Journal of Applied Behavioral Science*, Vol. 36, pp. 229-244.

Meadows D.H., Meadows D.L., Randers J. and Behrens W.H. (1972), *The limits to growth*. London: Pan.

Messner M. (2009), "The limits of accountability", *Accounting, Organizations and Society*, Vol. 34 No. 8, pp. 918-938.

Meyer J.W. (1986), "Social environments and organizational accounting", *Accounting Organization and Society* Vol. 11 No. 4/5, pp. 345-346.

Milne M.J. and Patten (2002), "Securing organizational legitimacy An experimental decision case examining the impact of environmental disclosures", *Accounting, auditing, & accountability Journal*, Vol. 15 No. 3, pp. 372-405.

Milne M. and Gray R.H. (2007), "Future prospects for corporate sustainability reporting", In Unerman J., Bebbington J. and O'Dwyer B. (Eds.), *Sustainability accounting and accountability*, Routledge Taylor and Francis Group, London, Uk, pp. 184-208.

Milne M.J., Tregidga H. and Walton S. (2009), "Words not actions! The ideological role of sustainable development reporting", *Accounting, Auditing and Accountability Journal*, Vol. 22 No. 8, pp. 1211-1257.

Milne M.J. and Grubnic S. (2011), "Climate change accounting research: keeping it interesting and different", *Accounting, Auditing & Accountability Journal*, Vol. 24 No. 8, pp. 948-977.

Milne M.J. and Gray R.H. (2013), "W(h)ither Ecology? The Triple Bottom Line, the Global Reporting Initiative, and Corporate Sustainability Reporting", *Journal of Business Ethics*, Vol. 118 No. 1, pp. 13-29.

Moneva J.M., Archel P. and Correa C. (2006), "GRI and the camouflaging of corporate unsustainability". *Accounting Forum*, Vol. 30 No. 2, pp. 121-137.

Morgan G. (1988), "Accounting as reality construction: Toward a new epistemology for accounting practice", *Accounting, Organizations and Society*, Vol. 13 No. 5, pp. 477-485.

Mumby D.K. (1987), "The political function of narrative in organizations", *Communications Monographs*, Vol. 54 No. 2, pp. 113-127.

Mumby D.K. (2004), "Discourse, Power and Ideology: Unpacking the Critical Approach", in *The SAGE Handbook of Organizational Discourse*, Ed. Grant and Hardy C. and Oswick C. and Putnam L., SAGE Publications Ltd, London, pp. 237-259.

Mumby D. and Clair R. (1997), "Organizational discourse", in Van Dijk T.A. (Ed.), *Discourse as social interaction*, SAGE Publications Ltd, London, UK, pp. 181-205.

Neu D., Warsame H. and Pedwell D. (1998), "Managing public impressions: environmental disclosures in annual reports", *Accounting, Organizations and Society*, Vol. 23 No. 3, pp. 265-282.

O'Connor E.S. (1995), "Paradoxes of participation: Textual analysis and organizational change", *Organization Studies*, Vol. 16 pp. 769-803.

O'Connor E.S. (2000), "Plotting the organization: The embedded narrative as a construct for studying change", *Journal of Applied Behavioral Science,* Vol. 36 pp. 174-192.

O'Dwyer B. (2002), "Managerial perceptions of corporate social disclosure: An Irish story", *Accounting, Auditing & Accountability Journal*, Vol. 15 No. 3, pp. 406-436.

O'Dwyer B. and Owen D.L. (2005), "Assurance Statement Practice in Environmental, Social and Sustainability Reporting: A Critical Evaluation", *British Accounting Review*, Vol. 37 No. 2, pp. 205-229.

O'Dwyer B., Unerman J. and Hession E. (2005), "User needs in Sustainability Reporting: Perspectives of Stakeholders in Ireland", *European Accounting Review*, Vol. 14 No. 4, pp. 759-787.

O'Dwyer B., Owen D. and Unerman J. (2011), "Seeking legitimacy for new assurance forms: The case of assurance on sustainability reporting", *Accounting, Organizations and Society*, Vol. 36 No.1, pp. 31-52.

O'Dwyer B. and Unerman J., (2016), "Fostering rigour in accounting for social sustainability", *Accounting, Organisation and Society*, Vol. 49, pp. 32-40.

Oswick C. (2000), "A dialogical analysis of organizational learning", *Journal of Management Studies*, Vol. 37 No. 6, pp. 887-901.

Oswick C., Keenoy T.W. and Grant D. (2000), "Discourse, Organizations and Organizing: Concepts, Objects and Subjects", *Human Relations*, Vol. 53 No. 9, pp. 1115-1123.

Owen G. (2013), "Integrated reporting: a review of developments and their implications for the accounting curriculum", *Accounting Education*, Vol. 22 No. 4, pp. 340-356.

Phillips N. and Hardy C. (2002), *Discourse Analysis – Investigating Processes of Social Construction,* SAGE Publications Ltd, London, UK, pp. 1-104.

Phillips N., Sewell G. and Jaynes S. (2008), "Applying critical discourse analysis in strategic management research", *Organizational Research Methods*, Vol. 11, pp. 770-789.

Putnam L. and Cooren F. (2004), "Alternative perspectives on the role of text and agency in constituting organizations", *Organization*, Vol. 11 No. 3, pp. 323-333.

Quattrone P. (2009), "We have never been Post-modern': On the Search of Management Accounting Theory", *European Accounting Review*, Vol. 18 No. 3, pp. 621-630.

Quattrone P. (2015), "Governing social orders, unfolding rationality, and Jesuit accounting practices: A procedural approach to institutional logics", *Administrative Science Quarterly*, Vol. 60 No. 3, pp. 411-445.

Quattrone P. (2017), "Embracing ambiguity in management controls and decision-making processes: On how to design data visualizations to prompt judgment". *Accounting and Business Research*, forthcoming.

Revellino S. and Mouritsen J. (2009). "The Multiplicity of Controls and the Making of Innovation." *European Accounting Review*, Vol. 18 No. 2, pp. 341-369.

Revellino S. and Mouritsen J., (2015), "Accounting as an engine: the performativity of calculative practices and the dynamics of innovation", *Management Accounting Research*, Vol. 28, pp. 31-49.

Roberts J. and Scapens R. (1985), "Accounting systems and systems of accountability – Understanding accounting practices in their organizational contexts", *Accounting Organizations and Society*, Vol. 10 No. 4, pp. 443-456.

Simnett R. and Huggins A.L. (2015), "Integrated reporting and assurance: where can research add value?", *Sustainability Accounting, Management and Policy Journal*, Vol. 6 No. 1, pp. 29-53.

Schiffrin D. (1994), *Approaches to Discourse*. Blackwell, Oxford.

Shapiro B.P. (1997), "Objectivity, relativism, and truth in external financial reporting: What's really at stake in the disputes?", *Accounting, Organizations and Society*, Vol. 22 No. 2, pp. 165-185.

Spence C. (2007), "Social and environmental reporting and hegemonic discourse", *Accounting, Auditing and Accountability Journal*, Vol. 20 No. 6, pp. 855-882.

Spence L.J. and Rinaldi L. (2014), "Governmentality in accounting and accountability: A case study of embedding sustainability in a supply chain", *Accounting, Organizations and Society*, Vol. 39 No. 6, pp. 433-452.

Solomons D. (1991), "Accounting and social change". *Accounting, Organizations and Society*, Vol. 16 No.3, pp. 287-295.

Stacchezzini R., Melloni G. and Lai A. (2016), "Sustainability management and reporting: the role of integrated reporting for communicating corporate sustainability management, *Journal of Cleaner Production*. Vol. 136 (Part A), pp. 102-110.

Stark D. (2009), *The sense of dissonance: Accounts of worth in economic life*, Princeton: Princeton University Press.

Stiglitz J.E., Sen A. and Fitoussi J.P. (2009), *Report by the Commission on the Measurement of Economic Performance and Social Progress* (CMEPSP), pp. 1-298.

The South African Institute of Chartered Accountants (SAICA), (2015), *Integrated Thinking: an exploratory survey*, pp. 1-41.

Thomas R., Sargent L. and Hardy C. (2011), "Managing change: negotiating meaning and power-resistance relations", *Organization Science*, Vol. 22, pp. 22-41.

Taylor J.R. and Van Every E.J. (2000), The Emergent Organization: Communication as Its Site and Surface, Mahwah, NJ: Lawrence Erlbaum Associates.

Taylor J.R. and Robichaud D. (2004), "Finding the Organization in the Communication: Discourse as Action and Sensemaking," *Organization*, Vol. 11, pp. 395-413.

Tregidga H. and Milne M.J. (2006), "From sustainable management to sustainable development: a longitudinal analysis of a leading New Zealand environmental reporter", *Business Strategy and the Environment*, Vol. 15 No. 4, pp. 219-241.

Tregidga H. (2007), *Power and Politics of Organisational Sustainable Development: An Analysis of Organisational Reporting Discourse*, a thesis submitted for the degree of Doctor of Philosophy at the University of Otago, Dunedin, New Zealand

Tregidga H., Milne M. and Kearins K. (2011), "Sustainable development as a floating signifier: Recognising space for resistance", Paper presented at the 10th Australasian CSEAR Conference, Launceston, Tasmania.

Tregidga H., Milne M. and Lehman G. (2012), "Analyzing the quality, meaning and accountability of organizational reporting and communication: Directions for future research", *Accounting Forum* Vol. 36 No. 3, pp. 223-230.

Tregidga H., Milne M. and Kearins K. (2014), "(Re)presenting 'sustainable organizations'", *Accounting, Organizations and Society*, Vol. 39 No. 6, pp. 477-494.

Tregidga H., Milne M. and Kearins K. (2018), "Ramping up Resistance: Corporate Sustainable Development and Academic Research", *Business and Society*, Vol. 57 No. 2, pp. 292-334.

UN (2012), *The Future we want: Outcome document of the United Nations Conference on Sustainable Development*, United Nations, Rio De Janeiro, pp. 1-73.

Unerman J. and Chapman C., (2014), "Academic contributions to enhancing accounting for sustainable development", *Accounting, Organizations and Society*, Vol. 39 No. 6, pp. 385-394.

United Nations Global Compact, (2011), *The Ten Principles*, pp. 1-41.

van Bommel K., (2014), "Towards a legitimate compromise? an exploration of Integrated Reporting in the Netherlands", *Accounting, Auditing & Accountability Journal*, Vol. 27 No. 7, pp. 1157-1189.

WCED (1987), "Our common future", World Commission on Environment and Development, Oxford University Press, Oxford.

Wertsch J.V. (1998) *Mind as Action*. New York: Oxford University Press.

Wodak R. and Meyer M. (2009), *Methods of Critical Discourse Analysis*, SAGE Publications Ltd, London, UK.

Wouters M. and Wilderom C. (2008), "Developing performance measurement systems as enabling formalization: A longitudinal field study of a logistics department", *Accounting, Organizations and Society*, Vol. 33 No. 4-5, pp. 488-515.

Wouters M. and Roijmans D. (2011), "Using prototypes to induce experimentation and knowledge integration in the development of enabling accounting information", *Contemporary Accounting Research*, Vol. 28 No. 2, pp. 708-736.

Yin R.K. (2004), *Case study research: Design and methods*, Sage Publications, Beverly Hills, CA.

Yongvanich K. and Guthrie J. (2006), "An extended performance reporting framework for social and environmental accounting", *Business Strategy and the Environment*, Vol. 15 No. 5, pp. 309-321.

Zappettini F. and Unerman J. (2016), "'Mixing' and 'Bending': The recontextualisation of discourses of sustainability in integrated reporting", *Discourse & Communication*, Vol. 10 No. 5, pp. 521-542.

For Product Safety Concerns and Information please contact our EU
representative GPSR@taylorandfrancis.com
Taylor & Francis Verlag GmbH, Kaufingerstraße 24, 80331 München, Germany

www.ingramcontent.com/pod-product-compliance
Ingram Content Group UK Ltd.
Pitfield, Milton Keynes, MK11 3LW, UK
UKHW022122190926
475702UK00013B/1589
9780367528119